How To Create Life:
Invent Plant And Animal Species That Really Fit Your World, A Reference For Writers, Gamers And Amateur Biologists!

AMY LAURENS

OTHER WORKS

SANCTUARY SERIES
Where Shadows Rise
Through Roads Between
When Worlds Collide
The Complete Sanctuary Series

KADITEOS SERIES
How Not To Acquire A Castle
How Not To Ring The Hero's Bell (2020)

STORM FOXES SERIES
A Fox Of Storms And Starlight (2020)

NON-FICTION
The 32 Worst Mistakes People Make About Dogs
How To Plan A Pinterest-Worthy Party Without Dying or Losing Your Chill

INKPRINT WRITERS SERIES
How To Write Dogs
How To Theme
How To Create Cultures
How To Create Life
How To Map (2021)

Find other works by the author at
http://www.amylaurens.com/books/

How To Create Life:
Invent Plant And Animal Species That Really Fit Your World, A Reference For Writers, Gamers And Amateur Biologists!

AMY LAURENS

Inkprint PRESS
www.inkprintpress.com

Copyright © 2019 Amy Laurens

All rights reserved. No part of this book may be reproduced in any form or by any electronic or mechanical means, including information storage and retrieval systems, without permission in writing from the publisher, except by a reviewer, who may quote brief passages in a review.

Print ISBN: 978-1-925825-88-6
eBook ISBN: 9781386381662

www.inkprintpress.com

National Library of Australia Cataloguing-in-Publication Data
Laurens, Amy 1985 –
How To Create Life: Invent Plant and Animal Species That Really Fit Your World, A Reference For Writers, Gamers and Amateur Biologists!
160 p.
ISBN: 978-1-925825-88-6
Inkprint Press, Canberra, Australia
1. Language Arts & Disciplines—Writing—Fiction Writing 2. Science—Life Sciences—Biology 3. Science—Life Sciences—Anatomy & Physiology

First Edition: November 2019

Summary: Learn how animals and plants adapt to their environments so you can convincingly invent your own.

Cover design © Inkprint Press.
Interior art © Amy Laurens
'Logarithmic chart of the hearing ranges of some animals' by Cmglee - Own work, CC BY-SA 3.0,
https://commons.wikimedia.org/w/index.php?curid=35890958

CONTENTS

Acknowledgements
Introduction   1

PART ONE: THE PLANT KINGDOM   3
Plant Types   4
Plant Bodies   10
Transpiration   18
Reproduction   22
Senses and Defences   31

PART TWO: ANIMALS   37
Carbon-Based Life   40
Musculoskeletal System   42
Heat Regulation and Water Loss   58
The Digestive System   66
Nutrient Circulation   77
Reproduction   84
The Senses   94

PART THREE: SMALL LIFE   113
Archaea   114
Bacteria   117
Protista (Including Algae)   120
Fungi   126
Viruses   130

Conclusion   134
References

ACKNOWLEDGEMENTS

How To Create Life is a stand-alone section from the forthcoming non-fiction work, *From The Ground Up*, a comprehensive worldbuilding guide covering everything from how to pick a star type for your planet to orbit, to how history influences beauty standards.

I would never have even attempted a work of such scope and ambition without the continued encouragement of Krista D. Ball, and I owe her a debt of gratitude.

I am also grateful to Margaret C., who spent hours combing over my early drafts, suggesting massive restructurings that have made this whole mess comprehensible for people outside my brain.

Immense thanks to Jess Ward, Mark Falkland, and Liana Brooks, all of whom loaned me their biological expertise in fact-checking and refining *How To Create Life*. This book would have been infinitely poorer without you, and far more riddled with errors. Thank you so, so much for your generosity and time in helping me to get as much of this right as I could.

Any remaining errors are, of course, all mine.

INTRODUCTION

The aim of this book is to help to build your own plants, animals, and other life—not because you need to start from scratch and reinvent every single living thing on your world, but because sometimes it's just plain fun to have a funky plant or animal that does what you need it to do.

Done well, invented plants and animals can lend colour and realism to a created world, and can even prompt new cultural developments for your people.

But done poorly, you can end up with plants or animals that will have savvy readers questioning what you were thinking.

So because plants and animals, just like people, are influenced by their surroundings, this book aims to give you the general principles of logic behind several key features of plant and animal biology. This will allow you to create life that doesn't just *exist* in its environment, but *flourishes*.

Firstly, we'll explore plant life:
- the general types of plants
- their physical structures
- how they 'breathe'
- how they reproduce
- their senses and defences.

Then we'll move on to animals, starting with a brief discussion of why Earth-based life is founded

on carbon and oxygen, and what other alternatives you might have. We'll cover:
- the musculoskeletal system
- heat regulation and water loss
- the digestive system
- nutrient circulation (breathing and blood)
- reproduction
- the senses.

Finally, we'll explore all those tiny things that are neither plant nor animal:
- archaea
- bacteria
- Protista (including algae)
- fungi
- viruses.

This will equip you with an excellent understanding of the basic logic behind the life forms you see around you, and the ability to extrapolate and design suitable life forms for any environment you might wish to create.

Have fun!

PART ONE
GREEN AND LEAFY: THE PLANT KINGDOM

While the term 'plant' might seem intuitive to most people, there's actually a lot of debate about what *exactly* a plant is.

For most of history, 'plants' were things that had cell walls made of cellulose (a type of carbohydrate) and got their nutrients via photosynthesis. They also produced embryos (think seeds and fruit).

However, some plant biologists are currently arguing that the term 'plants' should be expanded to include green algae as well, which photosynthesise and have cell walls made with cellulose.

Some biologists even think the term 'plants' should be applied to anything and everything that photosynthesises—certainly a simpler way to approach things!

But, regardless of what the biologists think, in this text we're going to look at algae later on in the section call *Tiny Life*. This section on plants will stick to the super-traditional definition, beginning with the main types of plants and then exploring the ways that a plant's environment can influence how it develops.

THE MAIN PLANT TYPES

A small percentage of the world's plants—around 7%—are nonvascular. 'Nonvascular' means that they don't have internal circulation systems, al-though a few have simplified versions. Nonvascular plants are liverworts, hornworts and mosses.

The remaining 93% of the world's plants are vascular plants, which means that they have a complex network of tubes (known as vascular tubes) designed to transport water and nutrients around their body.

Vascular plants can be further divided into seedless plants, which reproduce via spores, and seed plants, which create seed embryos packaged with nutrients inside a protective coating.

Seedless plants consist of club mosses, spike mosses, quillworts, ferns, whisk ferns and horsetails.

Seed plants are pretty much everything else, including flowering plants and conifers.

Of seed plants, flowering plants are by far the most common type of plant, making up nearly 87% of all known plant species, and are called 'angiosperms', because they make their seeds in reproductive organs. Flowers? Those are plant genitals. And fruit? Yeah, those are plant ovaries. Fun stuff.

Conifers, in case you were interested, are called 'gymnosperms', from the Greek *gymnos*, which means naked. This is because they *don't* enclose their seeds in reproductive organs, instead making them 'naked' on modified leaves (e.g. pinecones).

PLANTS: PLANT TYPES

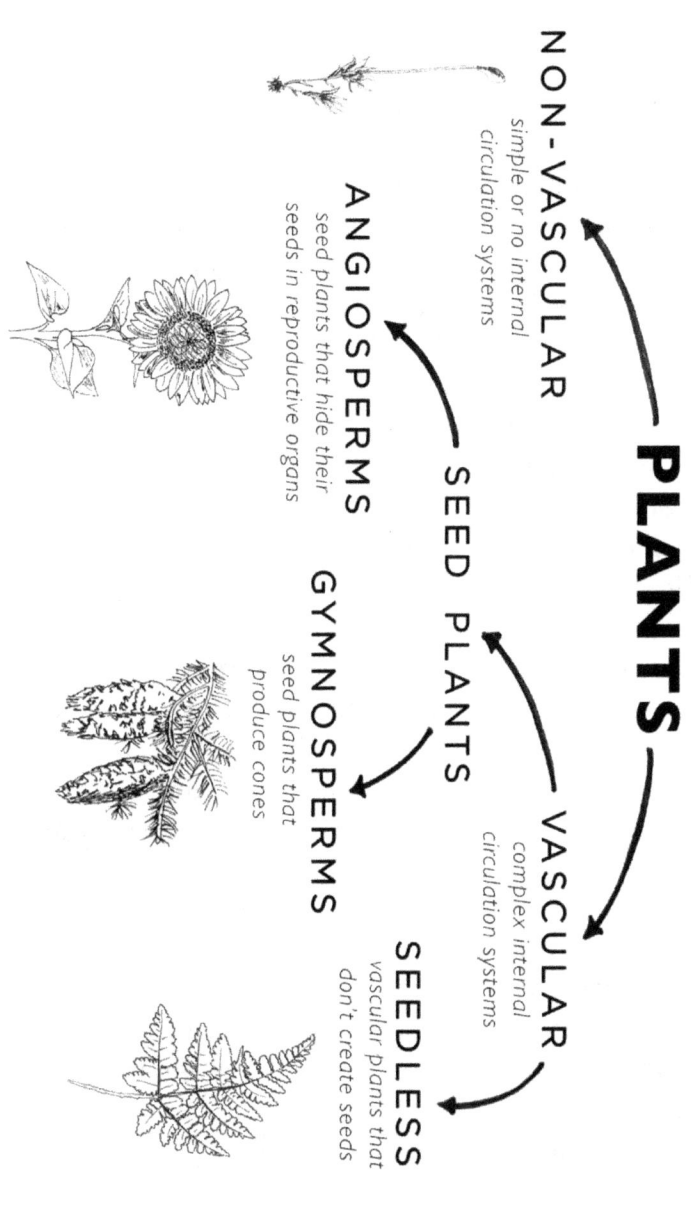

PLANTS

- **NON-VASCULAR** — simple or no internal circulation systems
- **VASCULAR** — complex internal circulation systems
  - **SEED PLANTS**
    - **ANGIOSPERMS** — seed plants that hide their seeds in reproductive organs
    - **GYMNOSPERMS** — seed plants that produce cones
  - **SEEDLESS** — vascular plants that don't create seeds

PLANTS: PLANT TYPES

A NOTE ON PLANT COLOURS

Most people know that it's chlorophyll that makes plants green. But why is chlorophyll green?

The short answer is because of the colour of sunlight. While the sun emits radiation across the whole colour spectrum, some of the visible light is absorbed by the atmosphere, and some is reflected away. The visible light that reaches the ground is mostly made up of red light, so, for photosynthesis to be optimally effective, it's important that plants can make use of this plentiful red light, absorbing as much of it as possible.

Blue light is also useful, even though there's less of it, because it's the most 'energetic' colour of light, providing the most energy to the plant.

So because of this, chlorophyll developed to maximise absorption of blue and red light. When blue and red light are absorbed out of the visible spectrum of sunlight, the leftover light—the light that the plant doesn't absorb, and that is bounced back for us to see—is green.

However, if plants formed on a planet that orbited a different type of star, the sunlight would be differently coloured.

On planets orbiting brighter, bluer stars, the vegetation would likely be yellow or orange—or possibly even bluish, if there was a lot of light, because blue light can cause something akin to sunburn in plants if they get too much of it.

PLANTS: PLANT TYPES

On a planet orbiting a cooler, redder star, the vegetation may be dark, possibly even black, as it strives to absorb all the red light.

FOR EXAMPLE

I'm going to work through this book as we go and create my own plant, animal and tiny life, just so you can see some of the possibilities.

I'm working with a section of land that I identified on the maps for *How To Map* (*Inkprint Writers* #5); you can see the relevant section on the next page. There are two continents—the land on the far left and far right respectively—and two islands, one small and one large. This is divided into three relevant countries, which you can see labelled 1, 2 and 3.

What is less clear from this map is that the large island is mostly mountains (there's a fault line running through it from left to right, more or less).

I also know that there's a major cold current in that northern bit of sea, while the southern bit of sea, below the island, is tropical.

So my first decision is what kind of plant I'll create. Because they're the most common type of plant, and because they're the type of plant that people interact with most, I'm going to be creating an angiosperm: a flowering, seed-producing plant. Keep reading for further details…

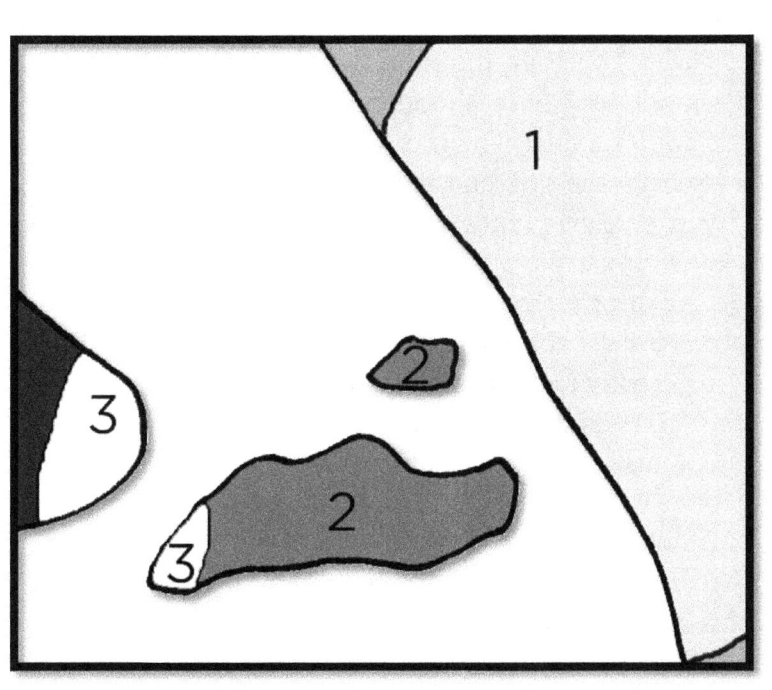

PLANT BODIES: THE PRIMARY ORGANS

Vascular plants, the ones with complex internal networks, have three main organs: roots, stems and leaves. Together, the stems and leaves are called the shoots, and both shoots and roots are vital for a plant's survival. The roots draw water and nutrients up from the soil, and the shoots provide energy and nutrients via photosynthesis.

Nonvascular plants are much simpler and don't have proper roots, stems or leaves. Their 'roots' don't really absorb water and nutrients very well, and are mostly just there for support.

Likewise, their 'leaves' aren't really leaves at all, but just green tissue that happens to be able to photosynthesise and that can directly absorb water (think mosses). Oddly enough, this actually makes them *less* likely to die of dehydration than plants with proper leaves, because they can survive on a lot less water.

However, because they can absorb water directly through their green tissue, they're very susceptible to pollution. This is why mosses are sometimes used as indicators of air quality: they're the first things to die off when the air goes bad.

Roots have three main functions: support, nutrition and storage. By burrowing down into the ground and spreading, roots anchor the plant against winds and other movement.

PLANTS: PLANT BODIES

These stabilising roots come in two general varieties: a taproot system, and a fibrous system.

Plants that form taproots have a single main root extending directly down into the soil, usually to a distance that's well over half of their above-ground height. From this single main taproot, other offshoots form, branching outwards in a pattern that mimics the branching pattern of many tall, single-trunked trees.

Generally speaking, seed-bearing plants, and plants that grow bark and wood (so not grasses, for example) use the taproot system, as it provides them with deeper stability and can counteract their weight. It also allows them to soak up water from deeper in the ground, so plants in dry or drought-prone areas often have taproots too.

Fibrous root systems, on the other hand, don't have a single taproot. Instead they're basically just a mat of thinner roots that's often quite shallow, although the root mats of some grasses (including wild wheat) can grow down even deeper than the height of the plant they're supporting. Regardless, they stabilise the plant because they're so dense.

They're still not as strong as taproots, though, so they're best suited to comparatively lighter plants, especially plants that don't grow wood or bark, such as grasses. Most seedless plants use root mats too.

These dense, fibrous root systems are actually very beneficial for the surrounding environment: as well as stabilising the plant, they also stabilise the

PLANTS: PLANT BODIES

topsoil. If topsoil doesn't have anything to anchor it, it can easily be blown or washed away—and the topsoil contains the most nutrients. If too much topsoil blows away, infertile dust bowls can result, causing famines and hardship for the people relying on the land. (Part of what led to the Great Depression in North America in the 1930s was erosion of the topsoil across large areas of farm land.)

As well as providing the plant with stability, roots play a vital role in nutrition. They absorb nutrients from the surrounding soil through their tips and can also store up these nutrients for the plant to use at a later date.

Did You Know?

Roots can also be aerial, as in the case of strangler figs, where they grow down to the ground in search of nutrients.

And some plants, such as maize, send out lateral growths that are actually stems, but that grow out from the plant and eventually down into the ground. These prop roots are unable to absorb nutrients like real roots, but, as their name suggests, they are there to prop up the plant and provide extra support.

Some roots can even grow upwards, as in the case of air roots, or pneumatophores, which allow plants such as mangroves to get oxygen from the air instead of trying to suck it in through thick, waterlogged mud.

PLANTS: PLANT BODIES

Sweet potatoes, carrots, beets and parsnips are just some examples of plants whose storage roots happen to be conveniently edible for humans. Left to their own devices, the plant will use up these stored nutrients when the plant flowers and reproduces—which is why, if you want to eat the storage roots or tubers, it's better to dig them before the plant begins to bud.

> ### Did You Know?
>
> Contrary to popular assumption, potatoes and ginger aren't actually roots. They're modified stems. Potato tubers are enlarged rhizomes, or horizontal underground stems. They don't absorb nutrients from the surrounding soil like roots do, but rather act as storage unit for nutrients. Ginger is exactly the same: we're not eating roots, but stems that grow underground and store nutrients.

Stems are segmented organs that allow the plant to:
- grow taller (getting closer to the sunlight and potentially outcompeting neighbours),
- increase rigidity (so they don't blow or get knocked over), and
- circulate nutrients and water.

At each of the joins between segments in the

stem, leaf buds can form. There's a particular pattern to how and when these leaf buds sprout, something that keen gardeners take advantage of when they prune plants.

Basically, the bud at the very tip of any branch (the terminal or apical bud) is the plant's priority: it's the first bud to grow, and it's where the plant will concentrate its efforts. Any other buds close to this bud generally won't sprout and grow—unless the tip bud is removed. Then you end up with a bunch of new tip buds, which all sprout and grow. This is why it's so effective to pinch out the tips of herbs if you want them to grow thick and bushy.

The terminal bud can only inhibit other buds within a certain range, though, so once the branch gets long enough, buds closer to the trunk will be able to sprout, becoming the terminal buds of their own, smaller branches.

Leaves, the organ that plants use to breath, have two parts: the flat blade and the central stalk that connects leaf to stem. This central stalk is known as the petiole.

Some plants, such as grasses, don't have a petiole, and their leaves connect directly to the stem, often wrapping around it and each other.

Some plants have one leaf per petiole, as in the case of oak trees, and some have multiple—like roses.

On the inside, leaves have vascular tissue, which transports nutrients and water around the plant in much the same way as the human circulatory system does (hence why the little lines down the blade of the leaf are called veins).

On the outside, they have a waxy coating known as the cuticle, which helps keep water in. The cuticle is usually thinner on plants that live in cool-to-warm wet climates where evaporation and water loss aren't so much of a problem, resulting in soft, fresh leaves. Plants in hot, dry climates have a thicker cuticle, resulting in stiff, dull or waxy leaves.

Did You Know?

Leaves can be modified by a plant in many different ways.

Onions, for example, are commonly considered a root vegetable, but like all bulbs are actually underground shoots that are mostly modified leaves. You can see this quite clearly if you cut an onion through vertically: small, thin roots hang from the bottom; a crunchy, tough, abbreviated stem forms above this; and modified leaves form the layers.

The tendrils on pea plants that allow them to climb are also modified leaves (unlike the curling tendrils of grape vines, which are stems), and the fleshy leaves of succulents are modified in order to retain water.

The spines of cacti are also modified leaves; the green, fleshy part of a cactus plant that performs photosynthesis is actually its stem.

PLANTS: PLANT BODIES

In conifers, the cuticles are extra thick to insulate the leaves from extreme cold, resulting in stiff, needle-shaped leaves that can survive being continuously frozen and defrosted during winter.

FOR EXAMPLE

The decisions I'm going to make as I build a plant species are going to be totally arbitrary, because I have no set goal in mind here other than 'create new plant that might be capable of creating story conflict'.

So, I'm going to pick a plant with a taproot, first of all, which means it's going to have a stem or trunk of some kind—not a grass.

I'm thinking a vine of some sort, because why not, so a long, main taproot, long, thin stems as the main branches of the vine, and the leaves—well, it looks like a lot of my action is going to take place in coastal regions or on the ocean, so my vine is going to be coastal, which means it needs moderately waxy leaves to keep fresh water in and to protect against the salt.

TRANSPIRATION: HOW PLANTS BREATHE

In general, when humans and animals breathe we call it 'respiration', because we take in oxygen and give out carbon dioxide and water. Plant breathing is called 'transpiration', because although it's a similar process, they take in carbon dioxide and give out oxygen and water.

In nonvascular plants, this process is a fairly basic gas exchange directly between the cells of the plant and the surrounding air (in fact, some mosses have 'leaves' that are only one cell thick). However, in vascular plants, leaves contain organs called stomata that allow them to perform this exchange.

In general, plant leaves have a high surface-to-volume ratio in order to maximise photosynthesis. However, this comes at a cost: the same surface-to-volume ratio that is helpful in maximising photosynthesis also means that they lose a lot of water through their leaves.

This is why plants need so much water. It's not like they're running around working up a sweat, but they do lose a significant amount of water every day just by breathing.

In hot, dry, windy conditions, leaves can lose more than their own weight in water in a day, and the sap delivering this water can travel as fast as the second hand traveling around a clock-face (about 75cm per minute).

PLANTS: TRANSPIRATION

In order to minimise this water loss when necessary, the plant can open and close its stomata, which are pores in the surface of the leaf. In general, plants that live in wet climates have more stomata on their leaves than those living in hot, dry climates, but intense light and low levels of carbon dioxide during the leaf's development can also increase the number of stomata a leaf develops.

A deficiency of carbon dioxide in the plant will also trigger the stomata to open, in much the same way as we would take a large breath if deprived of oxygen for a little while.

However, in general, stomata are open during the day, because even though they will lose water they can at least harvest energy through photosynthesis, and closed at night, because why waste water when you can't photosynthesise?

On the other hand, a lack of water can cause stomata to close even during the day, one key reason why droughts can significantly reduce cropping—the plant then receives fewer nutrients, and grows more slowly as a result, limiting the amount of crop it can bear within its life span. (Though droughts during flowering are problematic not because they force the stomata to close, but because the flowers make the plant keeps its stomata open, even when it is dehydrating.)

As well as stomata, some plants have special glands in their leaves that excrete salts. This is a particular adaptation of some plants in coastal conditions, which may not have access to fresh water. Whereas normal plants would curl up and die from the salt overload, plants with these special glands can open them when the leaf gets too full of salt, and the excess salts are pushed out, often forming a salty crust on the leaf.

> ### Did You Know?
>
> Xerophytes are a group of plants that have adapted to life in hot, arid climates. They have much smaller leaves, reducing the potential for water loss, and some have highly reflective leaves (for example, some species of eucalypts) or hairy leaves that trap a layer of water over them to help prevent water loss. These plants usually have most of their stomata on the underside of the leaves, unlike regular plants, which tend to have them on the top.

FOR EXAMPLE

The climate where my plant will live is mostly temperate and coastal, so the plant should get a decent amount of rainfall. This means it can afford to have a long, skinny stem with lots and lots of leaves on it, since it doesn't need to worry too much about losing too much water.

Because it's coastal, however, it will need to be adapted to salty winds and water. Some plants deal with this by secreting salt through their roots, but I like the idea of it secreting its excess salt through its leaves; maybe people will harvest the leaves as a source of flavouring in cooking.

Being a vine works in its favour as protection against wind too, as it will be able to cling to other plants and support structures to stablise itself.

REPRODUCTION: PLANT BABIES

The exact methods by which plants reproduce are pretty complex and technical, but most of us should remember the basics from high school: seed plants rely on pollination, with plants producing either male or female flowers or both, and pollinators such as bees transporting the pollen from the male flowers to the female flowers.

Non-seeding plants have a complex system that alternates between generations, with odd generations using asexual reproduction (the plant replicates itself in some way) and even generations using sexual reproduction (combining genes from two separate plants)—which could be fun to play with in worldbuilding if you're that way inclined.

However, here I'm going to concentrate on seeding plants, not only because they are the most numerous, but also because they are critically important to human survival, making up the bulk of our food.

Beyond the basics of pollination, the other important thing to bear in mind is in the analogies to animals: essentially, flowers are plant genitals, and fruit is plant ovaries, with the seed embryos nestled inside in much the same way as animal (and human) ovaries contain egg embryos.

I'll leave you to draw your own conclusions about the significance of the fact that a long-standing fea-

PLANTS: REPRODUCTION

ture of human courtship is the exchange of plant genitals (roses on Valentine's, anyone?), but the reason we eat plant ovaries is much more straightforward: because the plants want us to.

The entire point of making their 'ovaries' so sweet is to attract animals to eat them, because in the majority of cases the seeds are encased in hard, indigestible material that means they pass relatively unharmed from one end of the animal's digestive tract to the other.

This is an advantage to the plant, because the one thing plants need that they can't get for themselves is space. It's all very well to bear hundreds of seeds for new sunflowers, but if you're a sunflower yourself you don't actually want a hundred baby sunflowers trying to grow up around your feet, because you'll all be competing for nutrients and no one will end up thriving. So plant ovaries are tasty and sugary in order to entice other creatures to eat them and do the hard work of transporting the seeds on behalf of the plant: the plant gets to produce lots of babies and ensure its genetic line, but doesn't have to worry about competing with its children for resources.

So, why are there so many kinds of fruit, and how are they influenced by their environment?

Firstly, if you've ever tried to grow fruit yourself you'll know that there's a peak amount of water they need: the answer is definitely 'lots', but there's such a thing as overwatering too, which results in fruit that's so plumped up with water it's virtually

PLANTS: REPRODUCTION

flavourless (to wit, the rather disappointing rock melon we just harvested from our garden, which was so juicy I had to cut it over the sink, but contained very little flavour since it was so diluted by the water).

And in order to develop a really intense flavour, fruit also needs a lot of nutrition, which it gets from good quality soil.

But other than these two obvious factors, what determines the kind of fruit you'll get? Why do some fruits grow in temperate climates, and others in tropical environments?

In the most general of terms, the kinder the climate, the larger the fruit.

The vast majority of all fruit in the world (though not necessarily the kinds favoured by a western diet, which leans towards temperate fruits) thrive in tropical climates, where water is plentiful. These plants fruit at different times of the year in order to share out the pollination load: if the literally hundreds of flowering and fruiting plants in a tropical forest all flowered at once, there wouldn't be enough pollinators for all the plants to get the pollination they need.

Because of this, and because the climate is relatively stable all year round, the plants take it in turns, as it were; there's always *some*thing flowering or fruiting in a tropical forest or jungle, and some plants can fruit all year round (for example bananas, which are actually a type of large grass, not a tree).

PLANTS: REPRODUCTION

In contrast, most fruiting plants in temperate areas are deciduous in order to protect themselves from cold winters. Many insects also hibernate in winter to escape the cold, whic means that in spring there's a population explosion of pollinators, and the various plants respond by throwing out their flowers and fruit mostly at the same time as each other.

In even colder climates, plants can only grow fruit that ripens very quickly and doesn't need a long period of warmth. Additionally, most plants that are adapted to survive in really cold climates are conifers of some kind, which means they don't produce fruit at all, but rather produce seeds in cones.

So, in tropical areas you get fruit that grows slowly, takes time to ripen, and needs a lot of water. These fruits are also often more nutrient hungry; in the wild they get the extra nutrients required because they have more daylight hours in which to photosynthesise. There are literally hundreds and hundreds of fruits that thrive in the tropics, but ones common to the western diet include avocados, bananas, mangoes, lychees, coconuts, melons of all varieties, pineapples, passion-fruit, and more.

It's worth noting, though, that many of these will also survive in subtropical or even warm, humid temperate climates, so long as they don't get frost. It's not so much the excess of warmth as the lack of cold that makes these plants tropical natives.

In the subtropics, citrus fruit flourishes, because while citrus plants need a lot of sun and water, they

PLANTS: REPRODUCTION

don't like humidity—it results in poorer quality fruit, and the thick skins of citrus fruits succumb to mould too easily in humid environments.

In warm temperate areas you get the best of all worlds; as long as you protect tropical plants from possible frost, and as long as your stone fruit gets a cold-enough winter (although there are many varieties now known as 'low-chill', which can survive in warmer winters), you can pretty much grow anything.

In cool temperate climates, stone fruit (peaches, plums, cherries, apricots, etc.) and apples that require a cold period in order to kick-start their seeds into growing are the natives; berries also thrive in temperate areas.

Did You Know?

Botanically speaking, strawberries and raspberries are not actually berries, while bananas, tomatoes, pomegranates and kiwi fruit are!

Under this classification, a berry is a fleshy fruit without a stone which comes from a single flower that contains a single ovary.

Of course, the culinary definition is the one we tend to be more familiar with, and refers to small, pulpy, usually-edible fruits that are either sweet or sour and are usually quite juicy. In this text, 'berry' refers to the culinary version.

PLANTS: REPRODUCTION

In cold climates you get small, quick-ripening fruit, which is essentially limits the options to berries.

And of course, before you even get to fruit, you have flowers. Larger flowers require more energy to make, and also more water than smaller flowers. Because of this, it's likely that flowering plants in arid areas will have much smaller flowers than plants in tropical areas.

Colour is also affected by climate: there are three main pigments that plants use to colour their flowers, and each one reacts differently to heat.

Carotenoid pigments (like in pumpkins and carrots) create colours on the yellow-orange-red

---

Did You Know?

Carnivorous flowers (pitcher plants, Venus fly traps, and so forth) are usually found in bogs, because bogs are too acidic for nitrogen-producing bacteria, and the only other easy source of nitrogen is insects.

Sunflowers, orchids and peas make up 25% of all flowering plants.

Flowers from colder climates last better as cut flowers.

Bulbs need a period of cold before they will flower (which is why some retailers suggest keeping them in the fridge over winter if you live in a warmer climate) and so are mostly native to cold temperate and boreal forest biomes.

spectrum, and grow stronger when exposed to heat. For this reason, most tropical flowers are yellow, orange, red, or some variation on this spectrum.

Anthocyanin pigments (think 'cyan') create colours on the blue-purple-pink-red-black spectrum. Anthocyanins are fairly unstable and don't do so well in high heat, which is why tropical flowers in these colours are less common. However, anthocyanins respond well to cold, getting stronger and more intense, so flowers native to warm temperate areas are likely to be on the blue-purple-pink end of the spectrum, and flowers native to cold temperate climates are likely to be on the pink-red-black end of the spectrum.

Flowers that mostly use anthocyanins for their colouring can even change colour depending on the temperature, soil pH, and age of the flower. This is why the colour of many flowers fades as the flower ages; why hydrangeas flower either pink or blue depending on the pH of their soil; and why hibiscus plants can have different coloured flowers on the same bush.

Anthocyanins are also sensitive to sugar levels in the plant, so if the plant is well fed and healthy, its flowers will be brighter and more intense than if it's struggling for nutrients.

The final type of pigment is the flavonols. Like anthocyanins, they don't tolerate heat well and increase in both healthy plants and cold weather. Flowers that use flavonols for colouring are on the

PLANTS: REPRODUCTION

white-yellow spectrum—yellow if there are a lot of flavonols present (i.e. if the weather is really cold and/or the flower is really healthy) and white otherwise.

And of course, one plant can use a combination of these three pigments to achieve a certain 'look'; a common combination is anthcyanins with flavonols (since they're structurally quite similar) to get petals that are yellow or white around the edges, and pale to dark pink in the centre.

FOR EXAMPLE

Given that my plant is living in salty (i.e. harsh) conditions, it's not going to have large fruit for people to eat, and any fruit it does have are likely to be not only very small, but also tough and leathery rather than juicy since water loss is an issue.

I'm thinking I'll stick with the salty theme and, as well as the plant excreting excess salt through its leaves, have it store excess salt in its small black berries; many grazing animals like salty tastes (think about cows and horses around salt licks, for example), so having small, salty berries could be a good way for the plant to convince grazers to spread its seeds.

As a bonus, these can make a tasty addition to cooking for my people; it seems likely that the concentrated salt in the berries would impart a much stronger flavour than using the leaves, and given the berries are blue (a somewhat arbitrary decision, but we're in a warm climate so black is unlikely), they'll be chock full of antioxidants, too.

The compounds that make berries black also tend to make them high in vitamin C, in which case my little berries will not only be a great snack, they'll also make an excellent tonic for long-term travelling across the sea.

LIFE AS A PLANT: SENSES AND DEFENCES

Without going into all the chemical detail, suffice to say that although plants may lack sensory organs such as eyes and noses and tongues, they can still sense changes in their environments—sometimes even better than humans can.

In general, plants can sense changes in light, gravity, touch, temperature, salinity and moisture.

Plants are extremely sensitive to light (some individual plants have reacted to light levels the equivalent of no more than a second or two of moonlight when grown otherwise in darkness) and always tend to grow towards it. But what exactly are plants sensing when they sense light?

It turns out that plants are responsive to blue light and red light specifically and in different ways, as well as being responsive to the total amount of light they receive.

Exposure to blue light triggers a plant's photosynthesis reaction; it also slows the rapid growth of seedling stems once they breach the surface.

Exposure to red light, on the other hand, is what triggers seeds to germinate. Red light is also important because many plants use it to determine the length of a day—or, more properly, the length of a night. While some plants are day-neutral, meaning that they will flower when they reach a certain stage of maturity regardless of the seasonal light conditions, many plants can be categorised as either short-day or long-day plants.

Short-day plants will only flower when the daylight period is shorter than a certain length (the exact length is specific to the species).

Long-day plants will only flower when the daylight period is longer than a certain length (also specific to the species).

It's all very well, though, to say that plants grow towards the light—but what about a tiny seedling growing underground with no access to light at all? This example—supported by many scientific experiments—shows clearly that plants are also able to detect gravity, sending their roots down and their stems up.

Plants are also extremely sensitive to touch. We are intuitively aware that trees living on exposed, windy hillsides are likely to be shorter and have comparatively thicker trunks than trees of the same species living in more sheltered conditions, but plants are actually significantly more sensitive to touch than we might ordinarily imagine. In fact, they are so sensitive to touch that merely rubbing the stem of a plant twice a day can be enough to permanently stunt its growth.

Vines use this sense of touch to their advantage, with their grasping tendrils growing straight until they sense the touch of a potential support, which triggers a coiling response.

Still other plants, such as the Venus flytrap, use

PLANTS: SENSES & DEFENCES

this sensitivity to allow them to trap prey, with an electrical impulse akin to extremely slow nerve impulses travelling through the plant when one of its sensory hairs are touched.

Plants are also sensitive to a particular kind of touch by herbivores: being eaten. In response to this, plants have devised a wide variety of defence mechanisms. Many of these defence mechanisms are purely physical—for example, thorns and tough or spiky leaves—but some are chemical. Some of these chemical responses are straightforward, such as a bitter taste or toxic compound, but some are remarkably subtle. Two such defences are demonstrated by clover and maize.

Clover is commonly found in grazing lands. In order to avoid being over-grazed, clover has developed an extremely clever defence mechanism: it produces a hormone that mimics the effects of oestrogen in the mammal body, and production increases when the plant feels threatened.

The practical effect of this is that the more the clover is damaged (eaten), the more of this oestrogen-mimicking hormone it produces, and the more the fertility of its mammalian predators is affected—because an excess of oestrogen inhibits ovulation, much like the contraceptive pill. This means that fewer new predators are born next season, buying the clover time to regenerate—and once it is flourishing again, the concentration of the oestrogen-

PLANTS: SENSES & DEFENCES

Did You Know?

Our knowledge about plants' ability to react to their environments is still very incomplete. Take, for example, the Boquila vine from Chile, which can mimic the leaves of other plants. While plant mimics are not unheard of, the Boquila vine is totally unique (so far) because it can not only mimic another plant, but several all at once. One Boquila vine, it seems, is unlimited in how many different forms its leaves can take, and the form of its leaves seems to be entirely determined by the closest leaf of the plants around it—which means that one Boquila vine snaking its way through multiple other bushes can have leaves of numerous different shapes, colours and forms, all on the one plant.

Scientists have pretty much no idea how the Boquila vine can do this, but they're looking into gene transfer (although Boquila doesn't have to be touching another plant to mimic its leaves) and Boquila's ability to sense airborne chemicals secreted by nearby leaves (the equivalent of a plant sense of smell).

mimicking hormone decreases, and the sheep (or other mammalian predators) are free to reproduce as normal again.

Maize has as similarly clever defence system. When attacked by caterpillars, the combination of the destruction caused by the caterpillars' bites and a chemical compound in the caterpillars' saliva trigger the maize plant to release volatile compounds into the air. These compounds attract parasitic wasps, which then lay their eggs in the bodies of the attacking caterpillars. The eggs grow and hatch, killing the caterpillars and protecting the plant from further damage.

Interestingly, many plants also use this release of volatile compounds to 'warn' their neighbours of an infestation—in simple terms, it's reasonable enough to say that plants can smell when other plants of their species are sick and/or being predated upon (the two are often closely linked), and ramp up their own immune defences accordingly.

Plants are also responsive to temperature, changing their chemical structures and processes in response to hot and cold. Likewise, despite the fact that plants can't cope long term with extremely saline (salty) soil, most can adapt in the short term by altering their biochemistry.

Finally, plants are extremely sensitive to moisture levels, with too much water often drowning them (because water fills up in the soil spaces that usually allow the roots to access oxygen), and too little water both starving and dehydrating them. In response to a lack of water, most plants will close up their stomata (the little holes in their leaves through which they breathe), slowing water loss. This action causes the plant to wilt, something that's often accompanied by the leaves rolling in on themselves, which further decreases the chances of water loss.

FOR EXAMPLE

Ideally, at this point I want my plant to do something with its senses that increases conflict: something that makes it difficult for my people to get what they want, which apparently is the salty berries when they're in season, and the leaves otherwise.

The obvious solution is to make my salty vine (which really needs a name) a mimicking vine like Boquila. In season, the berries will be a give-away as to the vine's identity, but out of season it means people will have to search that bit harder to find the leaves they want for their cooking—particularly if I specify that the leaves only excrete salt on their undersides (harder to spot and plausible because plants often have their stomata on the underside of their leaves in harsh environments), and that there are several other plants in the area that can make people sick if they eat them.

The people will have to be extra careful to make sure that the leaves they collect are from the salty vine, and not from the toxic plants it mimics!

PART TWO
CLIMBING THE FOOD CHAIN: ANIMALS

As with plant life, the easiest way to go about populating your world with animal life is to simply copy a real-world biome. If this is even remotely feasible for your world, I recommend it as a way of avoiding the Black Hole of Worldbuilding Doom.

If, however, you would like to know how to create your own animal life—how the geography of a location influences the characteristics of its wildlife—this is the section for you.

May I suggest, though, that you stick to creating just one or two of each category of animal, only inventing more if your story particularly demands them; this gives the flavour of your unique world without miring you in work that is unlikely to be useful to the conflicts in your story.

Unless, of course, you're writing a conservation novel about the Royal Hteb Collector and her attempts to save the endangered species of the kingdom of Areik, particularly the illusive hteb—in which case go to town with the new species—but maybe include a glossary for all the unusual names!

Generally speaking, animal life on Earth can be split into two categories: vertebrates, which have a spine, and invertebrates, which don't. These are the two main categories we'll consider in the following sections when we look at the different factors that influence the 'design' of your animals.

Vertebrates (animals with spines) can be subdivided in many different ways, but for the purposes of this discussion we'll mostly look at them according to their eating habits because, as we'll see, a creature's eating habits significantly influence the way it adapts to its environment.

While we won't necessarily consider every possible diet in each section, this is the range of dietary possibilities we'll draw on:

- herbivores, which eat plant matter;
- insectivores, which eat insects and other invertebrates;
- omnivores, which are often scavengers and eat a wide variety of things; and
- carnivores, which eat exclusively or almost exclusively other vertebrates.

Invertebrates include insects, arachnids and crustaceans, as well as a host of water creatures such as jellyfish, shellfish, sea worms, cucumbers, stars, sponges, and much, much more. They too can be divided in terms of their eating habits, but because there are fewer options for movement, breathing, reproduction, and so forth when you are an invertebrate, eating habits have less of an impact on the creature's appearance than they do for vertebrates.

ANIMALS

Invertebrates vastly outnumber vertebrates on Earth, but they are often forgotten because they either live in the ocean (out of sight, out of mind), or are too small to draw much attention to themselves.

The following sections will look at the way that these different categories of animals do things like breath, digest food, reproduce, and so forth, and how these things affect their appearance.

Of course, if you have a magical world your animals can do anything and look any way you like—but as ever, it helps to know why things in our world work the way they do before getting creative.

Things are more spectacular, after all, when you understand *why* they're not ordinary.

CARBON-BASED LIFE

Before we get to animals in detail, I want to take a quick detour to look at the alternatives to carbon-based life.

All life on Earth is based on the element carbon; it forms long chains that are the backbone of all DNA. Most science fiction writers will have at least heard of stories where alternatives to carbon are used, and even in the fantasy genre it's common enough—popularised, perhaps, by Sir Pratchett's lovely interpretation of trolls as a race of silicon-based, moderately intelligent, mobile rocks in his *Discworld* series. But how plausible really is it to use something other than carbon?

The answer to this lies in the structure of carbon itself. A carbon atom can bond to four other atoms, which means it's very flexible and can make a wide variety of compounds. Silicon (and a few others) can do this too, but carbon is the smallest, so it forms compounds a bit more easily. And because it's lighter, the compounds carbon forms are lighter and more flexible: contrast carbon dioxide, which is a gas, with silicon dioxide (silicon being the next lightest element that can have four bonds), which is inflexible, unreactive, heavy—and it's also known as sand. Have you ever tried to breathe or digest sand?

Carbon is also special because it can form strong, stable double bonds with itself, which allows it to make the long, strong chains necessary for DNA.

CARBON-BASED LIFE

Silicon can form double bonds, but they're weak and unstable; sulphur can form long chains, but they're not as stable as carbon chains (though even on Earth some bacteria survive on sulphur rather than oxygen); and phosphorus can also form long-chain molecules, but it would have to be combined with nitrogen in order to make a wide enough variety of different molecules to facilitate all the different chemical processes required for life.

Of course, we don't really know what life that isn't carbon-based might look like, because it would have developed to suit conditions extremely different to Earth. For example, silicon compounds can't really move in normal Earth temperatures, but an extremely hot planet would allow them to be liquid or even gaseous, so it might work (though silicon-based life forms would still probably be crystalline in appearance).

THE MUSCULOSKELETAL SYSTEM: PHYSICAL APPEARANCE

And now on to creating your own animals! We're going to start with the skeleton and muscles, because this pretty obviously affects what your creature will look like.

You need a skeleton of some sort for all creatures, because without one, the creature would collapse under its own weight—although maybe you'd have other options here if you designed a planet with *significantly* lower gravity. However, 'skeleton' covers a wider range of options than you might think.

INVERTEBRATES

If you're looking to create an invertebrate, you have two options when it comes to skeletons: hydrostatic skeletons, and exoskeletons.

Hydrostatic skeletons are based on liquid rather than bones. Fluid is pressure-sealed in chambers in the body, and the creature uses its muscles to move this pressurised fluid chamber in pretty much the same way we use our muscles to move our bones.

However, the types of movements creatures with hydrostatic skeletons can make are much more limited, since the fluid chambers can't form shapes as complicated as bones can. Also, the fluid chambers aren't as strong as other types of skeletons, so the size of creatures with hydrostatic skeletons is limited—unless you were, perhaps, on an ocean planet, or a planet with significantly lower gravity, as either of these options would reduce the pressure demands on the hydrostatic skeleton and thus allow the creature to grow larger.

In keeping with this, creatures on Earth with hydrostatic skeletal systems are mostly (though not exclusively) aquatic: corals, jellies, hydras, flatworms, roundworms, and segmented worms.

Exoskeletons are more familiar: this is some sort of hard protection on the outside of the animal. Shellfish are an obvious example, using calcium carbonate that is secreted by their mantles (in much the same way our noses secrete mucous) to create a protective shell around them, which they can add to as they grow.

Alternatively, you can have jointed exoskeletons like those of insects and arachnids. These exoskeletons are made out of 'cuticle', a non-living covering secreted by the skin of the creature (sort of like how our fingernails are non-living coverings over our skin). Between a third and half of this cuticle consists of a material called 'chitin', a carbohydrate similar in structure to plant fibre that's also an important component in mushrooms and other fungi.

Although it's somewhat trendy, especially in science fiction, to create giant, bug-like aliens with exoskeletons, sadly, this isn't really feasible (sorry,

ANIMALS: APPEARANCE

Shelob and Aragog). The biggest barrier to size lies in the types of joint available with an exoskeleton. Because they can't be supported by ligaments, tendons and cartilage (otherwise the skeleton would no longer be exo-, or external), exoskeletons have pin joints—and they are fairly weak. They concentrate all the weight of the limb and all the force of any movement into a tiny area, so they can't bear very strong loads.

Exoskeletons are also problematic because they're not as strong as bones, and they don't repair as easily or quickly as muscles do.

Because of all this, creatures with exoskeletons can't actually grow very big at all: the Japanese spider crab is the largest creature with an exoskeleton, with a leg span of approximately 3.65 metres, or 12 feet, and the American lobster is the heaviest, clocking in at 20kg or 44lbs.

In fact, the lobster provides an excellent example of the size barrier for exoskeletal creatures, because lobsters don't actually die of old age. Bear with me as I explain.

As far as we can tell at the moment, the key cause of aging is the gradual wearing away of our telomeres, the sections of repetitive sequences at the end of our DNA strands. These telomere sections protect the DNA that actually carries our genetic information from deteriorating or fusing with neighbouring DNA, but they break down over time—causing aging.

ANIMALS: APPEARANCE

Lobsters' telomeres don't degrade over time—which is to say that, as far as we can tell, lobsters actually do not age. They are not immortal, however, because exoskeletons are inflexible: they don't grow.

If you have an exoskeleton, you have to shed it periodically as the squishy parts of your body outgrow the rigid container they live in. This process is both costly in terms of energy resources—you have to grow an entire new exoskeleton—and dangerous, in that it leaves you very vulnerable to predation in the in-between stage.

And because you are growing larger and larger exoskeletons, they become more and more costly in terms of energy to grow. This places a natural size limit on an creature with an exoskeleton: the size at which it can no longer consume sufficient nutrients to make growing a new exoskeleton worthwhile.

And thus, we have the lobster, who eventually gets big enough that it can't grow itself a new skeleton, but which never stops growing internally. Instead, they succumb to exhaustion, predation, and shell failure as the exoskeleton is damaged or becomes affected by moulds and loses structural integrity.

All excellent reasons why giant bugs (I'm sorry) are physically and practically implausible.

Of course, you could always create a creature that used both an internal skeleton *and* an exoskeleton (see for example the Formics, or 'Buggers', in *Ender's Game*).

ANIMALS: APPEARANCE

VERTEBRATES

Vertebrates have an endoskeleton ('endo' meaning internal): hard, supporting elements (usually bones) encased by soft tissue.

Basically, we're looking at bones bound together by protein fibres, known as muscles, ligaments or tendons depending on how the protein fibres are arranged. There's probably also some cartilage (another type of protein) thrown in there somewhere for good measure and extra support, such as in human knees.

The most obvious factor that determines what shape a creature's skeleton will be is how it moves—skeletons for creatures that swim (like fish) need to be very different to skeletons for creatures that walk—so we'll look at skeletons firstly for creatures that swim, then for creatures that fly, and then for creatures that walk and run.

The size and eating habits of the creature are the other two things that determine what its musculo-skeletal system will look like, and we'll consider those after.

Most vertebrates who spend their entire life **swimming** are some variety of fishy creature, and don't have limbs (because they don't need them to swim, and unnecessary limbs mean extra, unnecessary joints, which make it easier for the creature to be injured). Instead, their skeleton is quite basic, with just a skull, spine, and ribs. (The exception to this is mammals, who have front

ANIMALS: APPEARANCE

Did You Know?

Eating habits also impact a creature's social structure. Carnivores require a lot more calories than herbivores, so it takes a lot of herbivores to sustain just a few carnivores. Because of this, and because flocking together in large numbers is also a great form of protection, herbivores who might make a tasty snack for a carnivore often have large social groups—schools of fish, flocks of birds, herds of cattle, etc.

Carnivores, on the other hand, are more likely to be solitary. Of course, hunters can also form packs—see wolves, lions, and even dolphins. It's thought, though, that because hunting is something that requires the coordination of lots of complex skills, hunting creatures are therefore smarter than prey creatures and probably have much more complicated social rules and boundaries.

This sort of thing is hard to study quantitatively though, and scientists still can't agree on the criteria for an animal being considered 'smart', so you can probably take or leave this as you choose.

limbs—flippers. This is assumed to be because mammals first occurred on land before returning to the water.)

For these creatures, eating habits are more important than size in determining their final shape.

ANIMALS: APPEARANCE

Herbivores, who graze on plants and algae, don't need to chase down their nutrients or rely on cunning in order to eat. Because of this, they tend to have shapes designed to increase stability at slow speeds: narrow, upright figures so they don't tumble sideways in the ocean currents, with broad fins and tails for balance.

Carnivores, on the other hand, with their obvious need for speed, trend towards a rounder, torpedo shape with narrow fins and tails that allow them to cut quickly through the water and turn agilely.

Unlike eating habits, size is less limiting in the ocean: buoyancy helps to combat the effects of gravity and makes it easier to grow big.

However, even ocean creatures have size limits, for reasons that we will explore when we look at the other parts of the animal; it seems that blue whales, at about 33 metres or 110 feet long, and 180 or more tonnes, are pretty much as big as you can get. Even dinosaurs couldn't make it past these dimensions; although a few species may have beat the blue whale for length, they didn't come close in terms of mass.

Unlike creatures that swim, **flying** creatures obviously *do* have limbs—wings and legs—and their skeletons will be shaped accordingly. Weight is also an issue with flying creatures, because if they're too large and heavy they won't be able to get themselves off the ground.

One way that flying creatures compensate for that is by having hollow bones. However, this can only

ANIMALS: APPEARANCE

compensate so far; the common idea of a human-sized creature with angel wings is actually physically impossible, because the angel would need a chest three times bigger than an average man in order to house its ginormous pectoral muscles. Which, okay, that could happen, even if it would look a bit odd—but it would create a new problem, because all that muscle mass is heavy, so the angel would need even more muscle to lift the other muscle, and so on and so forth.

And sadly, because the ratio between mass and power is exponential rather than linear, you can't just scale up an eagle and create a plausible massive bird either. Thus, much like the poor lobster who eventually cannot grow a shell big enough for itself, there is a natural weight limit on flying creatures as well. The largest flying creature is thought to have weighed only about 81 kilos, or 180 pounds (though of course, you could presumably go bigger than this if your gravity was weaker).

Carnivores will need power, speed and agility, and often spend significant proportions of their time soaring (riding thermal currents in the air) to conserve energy; herbivores and insectivores, on the other hand, tend to be smaller and rounder, with shorter wings proportionate to their body size that allow them to make rapid, agile movements for long periods of time.

Leg and beak size are also determined by a bird or bird-like creature's eating habits; there isn't the

ANIMALS: APPEARANCE

space here to cover every variation possible, but consider the kind of food your birds will be eating. Are they cracking nuts (strong, thick beak required), picking berries from amid thorns (long, thin beak required), wading for aquatic insects or amphibians (long and thin, spoonbill-shaped, or even pouched like a pelican to filter food), catching fast-moving insects (strong and grippy but not chunky or unwieldy), and so forth—and think about what kind of beak and legs they would need to best achieve this.

Finally, the least efficient way of moving: **walking** and running. I mentioned just before that the muscle power needed to lift a creature gets exponentially larger the heavier the creature is; the size of the legs needed to support a walking or running creature show the same relationship.

This is why a mouse can have tiny, skinny little legs while an elephant must have thick, stumpy ones; if you were to scale a mouse up to elephant size, its legs would break under the strain of holding up its own weight.

There's another factor too: posture. Legs that are directly under the main weight of the body allow the supporting muscles and tendons to bear a lot of the load, which means the creature can be bigger without having to have proportionately massive leg bones. But large animals have four legs underneath them for a reason, and that's for stability and strength. Sorry, *Jurassic Park* film: your Brachiosaurs really couldn't lean back on their hind legs to reach leaves, because

ANIMALS: APPEARANCE

Did You Know?

> If you're going to start creating your own animals, it's worth bearing in mind the importance of consistency. Unless you are going to come up with a whole evolutionary scheme in support of your creatures, they are probably going to have to slot in with Earth-like creatures, which means conforming to Earth-like patterns.
>
> Sorry, *Avatar* directors: this makes it extremely unlikely that you will have four-limbed birds, four-limbed sentients, and six-limbed everything else!
>
> Consistency aside, four is an ideal number of limbs: it maximises stability while minimising vulnerability, as joints are the weak points in the skeleton and more joints means more susceptibility to injury.
>
> On the other hand, the likelihood of all aliens having evolved to look basically humanoid is really very low; since humans are uniquely adapted to Earth-like conditions, if you throw in a bunch of humanoid aliens you're essentially assuming the life only exists on Earth-like planets. Diversity of alien life forms is something that the modern *Dr Who* series manage pretty well, though mostly in the Eccleston and Tenant eras.

those hind legs would break.

In short: the bigger the creature, the more likely it is to have legs that are set directly under it to

ANIMALS: APPEARANCE

support its body weight, rather than, say, reptile-like creatures that have legs set out to the side of the body. Sadly, this also makes giant lizards a physical impossibility, which means no dragons, which are usually depicted across cultures as reptilian creatures with legs set out to the side, rather than directly underneath them, meaning that their shoulder and hip joints couldn't physically support the dragon's weight—although dragons are generally magical creatures, so you can probably hand wave any problems with their physics away anyway!

Dexterity is also a factor of a creature's size and skeletal configuration: human arms have a much greater range of movement than human legs because they're not load bearing and so don't need to be as stable. Contrast this with a creature that is big and heavy and needs all four of its limbs to bear its weight—they have no limbs left over to be flexible and dextrous. So, medium to small creatures are more likely to be dextrous than big creatures—though of course you can get creative, as with the elephant, which uses its nose as a flexible, dextrous fifth limb.

The ability to walk upright also changes a creature's skeleton: the position of the skull on the neck is relatively more upright, and the sacral vertebrae (the final vertebrae that brace the spine against the pelvis and lower limbs) fuse together (called the sacrum) in order to prove rigid support for the pelvis and legs. Birds' spines do this as well.

ANIMALS: APPEARANCE

They have even *more* vertebrae fused together, which suggests that flying requires even more spinal stability than walking.

Finally, the eating habits of a walker or runner will also affect the shape of its skeleton. As with swimmer and flyers, carnivores are going to need speed and power in order to capture prey, and this again limits their size. Above a certain mass, the frame needed to provide enough power leads to the same paradox as with the flyers: more mass requires exponentially more power to move, which requires more muscle, which creates more mass.

Because of this, major predators that rely on speed to catch their prey top out with some of the mid-sized dinosaurs in the past, and with lions, tigers, bears, saltwater crocodiles, sharks and orcas today.

In contrast, herbivores spend the majority of their time eating, and although speed may be necessary to outrun a predator, they tend to rely more on numbers for protection, so their frames can be comparatively bulkier than those of predators from a similar climate (although plenty of herbivores do rely on speed as well, such as antelopes).

Omnivorous creatures can sit somewhere in the middle, but it makes a difference whether they hunt their food or just scavenge for it.

Creatures that hunt other animals for food (whether carnivore or omnivore) usually have forward-facing eyes for depth perception and tools such as claws and teeth to help them catch their food.

ANIMALS: APPEARANCE

Animals who scavenge for their meat, or who ambush their prey rather than hunting it down, vary in terms of their appearance; depth perception is not so important, though teeth to tear meat will still be a required, and claws are an optional extra.

Herbivores on the other hand—and especially herbivores that are eaten by predators—often have side-set eyes in order to maximise their range of vision; being able to calculate exactly how far away a

> ### Did You Know?
>
> Marine mammals tend to live in colder waters as these waters have higher nutrient levels. Tropical waters are usually clear waters, and clear waters are nutrient-poor.
>
> Tropical waters have higher levels of speciation (number of unique species), but this is precisely *because* of the comparatively low level of nutrients, promoting specialisation so species don't compete with each other.
>
> The lower levels of nutrition in tropical waters, caused by lower levels of oxygen and carbon dissolved in the warmer waters, means less phytoplankton, which means less animal life in general—which also means fewer predators. This is why whales and other aquatic mammals often give birth in tropical waters: the mother effectively starves for a few months while the baby grows, but on the other hand, there are virtually no predators to threaten the baby.

ANIMALS: APPEARANCE

predator is with your superior depth perception isn't as important as being able to see that the predator is there in the first place.

FOR EXAMPLE

Looking at the map (back on p9), it's pretty clear that the sea is going to play an important role in this story world of mine, so I'm going to focus on creating a sea creature.

Because I also want to be able to demonstrate some of the complexities of animal creation, I'm going to go with a vertebrate, rather than an invertebrate. Invertebrates can do all sorts of cool things too, but the options you have for things like digestion and reproduction are much more limited.

So I'm looking at a swimming vertebrate—most of which are fish, but there are a few mammals and reptiles and things in there as well, and although my husband is a mad keen fisherman and I can appreciate a pretty fish as well as anyone, I really do prefer mammals. So for no reason other than person bias, it's going to be a swimming *mammal*.

I have no set ideas about what I want this creature to do yet, so let's brainstorm some ideas for conflict.

I know I'm going to need people travelling by sea using some form of magically-powered transport (because I prefer writing fantasy stories—again, this is just personal bias).

The seas in which they will mostly travel will be full of cold currents, and is relatively close to the north pole.

Not entirely coincidentally, most marine mammals live in colder oceans, so that's satisfactory.

In order to create conflict, I need some sort of sea mammal that can a) live in cold oceans and b) cause trouble for the people trying to travel there.

I *could* take the easy route and assume that the creature causes trouble because it's a valuable resource that people fight over (think walrus or narwhal tusks), but in the interests of keeping myself on my toes, I want something that's going to cause direct conflict with my people.

Either the creature can be after the people themselves (to eat, or simply to scare them away from breeding grounds, nurseries, etc.), or it can interfere drastically with the people's mode of transport.

The latter is a little more original and a little less KILLER SEA CREATURES ARE OUT TO EAT YOU cliché, so let's run with that.

...Which basically tells me nothing about what this creature's diet is going to be, so the exact form of its body is still uncertain. It's a swimming mammal, which means it has a skull and spine plus limbs, presumably flippers, and a tail.

Let's leave the exact form undecided for now, and see what we discover as we look at the other characteristics of animals.

HEAT REGULATION AND WATER-LOSS: MAINTAINING A STABLE BODY CLIMATE

When it comes to maintaining body temperature, it turns out that bigger is definitely better. The bigger the creature, the lower its surface-to-volume ratio is (less skin per unit of internal *stuff*), which means it doesn't lose heat or water as quickly as a small creature, whose surface-to-volume ratio is high (lots of skin/surface area per unit of internal matter).

There's one other factor that influences heat and water loss: where the creature gets its heat from. In old terms, we're talking cold- or warm-blooded. However, because the blood of cold-blooded creatures can actually get *hotter* than the blood of warm-blooded creatures, scientists have changed the terms. Officially, we now talk about creatures that are endothermic (endo meaning internal), who can generate their own heat, and creatures that are ectothermic (ecto meaning external), who need to absorb heat from their surroundings.

INVERTEBRATES (AND OTHER ECTOTHERMS)

Most invertebrates are ectotherms, meaning they have to rely on their surroundings for heat. Fishes, amphibians and reptiles are also ectotherms. Most

ANIMALS: HEAT & WATER LOSS

people are aware of this in general terms—think of the familiar image of snakes and lizards sunning themselves in order to warm up in the morning.

The reason that these creatures can't keep themselves warm is because their metabolisms run too slowly; their hearts beat slower, they breathe more slowly, and they don't absorb nutrients as quickly as endotherms. As a trade-off, however, they require far fewer nutrients and can survive on far fewer calories, because they don't need all those extra calories to regulate their body temperature.

Ectotherms are able to survive a much wider range of temperatures than endotherms—one of the key reasons why the term 'cold-blooded' is so misleading, since under the right conditions an ectotherm's blood can actually get hotter than an endotherm's. However, they still have an optimal range that they try to maintain.

Aquatic ectotherms, including all the invertebrates and also most fish, are at the mercy of the surrounding water when it comes to maintaining their body temperatures—usually their body temperature is within a couple of degrees of the surrounding water.

Ground-dwelling ectotherms (insects, other invertebrates, amphibians and reptiles), on the other hand, can modify their body temperature by changing their behaviour. Most obviously, they can move from a hotter area to a cooler one, or vice versa. Many ground-dwelling ectotherms spend their day chasing

ANIMALS: HEAT & WATER LOSS

sunlight in order to maintain a stable body temperature; insects, particularly, will often spend the night somewhere they can be assured of getting sun first thing in the morning in order to raise their body temperature enough for them to become active.

Insects also use their posture to maximise or minimise exposure to the sun, depending on whether they are trying to heat up or cool down. In hot weather, flying insects will minimise movement (flying generates a lot of heat in the flight muscles).

Some amphibians, such as bullfrogs, can vary the amount of mucous they secrete from their skin in

Did You Know?

Honeybees have some particularly noteworthy behaviours designed to help them regulate temperature. In hot weather, they can be seen transporting water to the hive, where they will dump it in pools. They then fan these pools with their wings, encouraging evaporation and convection to help cool down the hive.

In cold weather, the bees huddle together for warmth, taking turns at being on the colder outer edge and using their stashes of honey as energy to help their metabolisms run faster. Queen bees use the heat generated by flapping their wings to keep their eggs warm, transferring the heat from their flight muscles to their abdomen, which they then press against their eggs like a live hot water bottle.

ANIMALS: HEAT & WATER LOSS

order to cool down faster (similar to how our bodies use sweat).

Being ectothermic means that these creatures are tied closely to their environment—something which influences their size. Numerous studies have shown that ectothermic creatures grow more slowly in colder climates, likely because their metabolisms don't get the extra heat energy to speed them up that creatures in hotter climates get.

However, ectothermic creatures in colder climates tend to grow bigger overall than ectothermic creatures in hotter climates. This is related to what I said about surface-to-mass ratios: the bigger the creature is, the less quickly it loses heat, so being big is an advantage in cold climates where you need to conserve as much heat as possible, and being small in hot climates is an advantage because it's easier to stay cool.

(ENDOTHERMIC) VERTEBRATES

Most vertebrates, including birds, are endotherms, meaning they generate their own body heat. Being endothermic has distinct benefits: an endothermic creature doesn't have to rely on its surroundings to maintain a consistent body temperature.

However, it does use more energy than an ectothermic creature. An endotherm's metabolism is faster than that of an ectotherm: its rate of digestion is faster, it breathes more quickly, and its heart beats

ANIMALS: HEAT & WATER LOSS

faster. Because of this, endothermic creatures generally consume more calories—but they're also more suited to long, continuous periods of movement (long distance running, or flapping in order to fly, for example) because they breathe faster and so can keep up their oxygen supplies better.

Endotherms can also live in a much wider range of habitats than ectotherms because they can regulate their body temperatures; only a tiny handful of ectotherms can survive in the below-freezing temperature of polar water, but many endothermic species thrive there.

> ### DID YOU KNOW?
>
> While cool technology such as shoes that charge your phone while you walk are definitely in the works, it's important to note that these sorts of devices are generating energy from movement, not from the inherent energy of the humans wearing them.
>
> I love *The Matrix*, and in high school I could quote most of the script, but growing humans in stationary pods to harvest electricity from them? The machines would have been better off clothing them in battery cloth and making them run around playing basketball, because lying static as they were, it would have taken more energy to keep the humans alive than the machines could possibly have harvested from them.
>
> The joys of being an endotherm.

ANIMALS: HEAT & WATER LOSS

So what makes an endotherm an endotherm?

One of the crucial elements they need is insulation, something that keeps all that heat they're generating inside their body. Skin, fat layers and hair or fur or feathers are the best forms of insulation.

Skin is obviously important because it's a physical barrier between the inside of the creature and the outside.

Fat layers are highly effective insulators, because it's difficult for heat energy to pass through fat. In fact, fat is such a good insulator that human babies are born with 'brown fat' deposits all over their body. This brown fat disappears as they get older, and its entire purpose is to help keep the baby warm until its brain learns to regulate its temperature better. Fat deposits are also why so many marine endotherms have a rounded, blobby sort of shape: think seals, whales, penguins, walruses, etc. A lot of insulation is needed to regulate body temperatures in the freezing polar waters.

Hair, fur and feathers all work as insulators because air is actually not a great conductor; it takes quite a lot of energy to heat up air, which is why home heating bills can be so large during winter. When hairy, furry or feathery creatures get cold, they often raise up their hair, fur or feathers in order to trap air against their skin, forming an additional layer of insulation. This is why we get goose bumps.

In some creatures that are especially adapted for cold weather, a second, outer layer of hair, fur or

ANIMALS: HEAT & WATER LOSS

features covers the softer inner layer. This outer layer of guard hairs or feathers protects the softer undercoat from getting wet or dirty, both of which inhibit its ability to trap air and thus insulate.

So: if your creature lives in a cold environment, they are probably going to have significant deposits of fat, or a double layer of hair, fur or feathers to keep them warm (or both!).

But what about creatures who live in hot climates? These creatures obviously don't have to worry so much about keeping warm as they do about staying cool.

Unlike air, water is a really good conductor of heat, so most land animals lose heat either by sweating or by panting. Both work on the same principle: bodily fluid that's mostly water is exposed to the air, and it evaporates, creating a cooling effect.

Generally speaking, the hairier (or more feathery) a creature is, the more they will pant and the less they will sweat, as sweat would destroy the insulation that their hair (or feathers) provides (which can help to keep heat out, as well as keep it in). Some creatures, like dogs, sweat through their paws as well as panting, and some, like birds, might splash around in water to cool down. Some, like rodents and kangaroos, also lick themselves (particularly their arms, where their skin is thinner) to cool down.

FOR EXAMPLE

My creature is a swimming mammal, so clearly, being mammalian, it's endothermic and generates its own heat source.

In the cold polar seas, this means that it's going to need to move a lot to keep warm—which means consuming more calories!—and that it will probably need a layer of fat (blubber) to help it stay warm and insulated in the cold water.

A thick double-coat of fur or hair will also be necessary to keep it warm.

...Can you see how we're slowly eliminating options for its physical appearance simply by considering what we need the creature to do? This is why I wasn't too concerned about pinning down its specific form in the last section.

THE DIGESTIVE SYSTEM: OBTAINING NUTRIENTS

There are two types of chemicals that animals need to digest from their food in order to survive:
- the raw materials for building new cells: carbohydrates (including sugars), lipids (also known as fats) and proteins; and
- essential nutrients (amino acids, fatty acids, vitamins and minerals).

Although it seems obvious that a big creature needs to eat more than a small creature, in actual fact bigger creatures need fewer calories proportionately. Every gram of mouse, for example, requires about 20 times the calories as a gram of elephant. The reason for this relationship is not entirely clear; there is some relation to heat loss and surface-to-mass ratios, but there is still more to the story that scientists have as yet been unable to tease out.

INVERTEBRATES

Invertebrates can digest things in two main ways. The first, found in flatworms and cnidarians (hydras, jellyfish, coral, anemones, etc.), is the gastrovascular cavity system (described in more detail in the following chapter on circulation).

Essentially, a gastrovascular cavity system is just a large cavity or series of cavities inside the body

ANIMALS: DIGESTIVE SYSTEM

where the surrounding water (or occasionally air) can enter the body of the organism and deliver nutrients and gases directly to the majority of the creature's cells.

The other option is a highly simplified version of the digestive tract of vertebrates, often nothing more than a closed-off tube extending from one opening to another (unlike the gastrovascular cavity, which only has one opening through which food is brought in, and waste expelled). The advantage of a simplified digestive tract over a gastrovascular cavity is that food travels through the tube in only one direction, so the creature can capture ('eat') more food before earlier meals have finished digesting. This is better for creatures whose food supply comes in fits and starts, rather than a constant stream.

VERTEBRATES

Generally speaking, vertebrates digest things the same way invertebrates do: there's a tube, it goes from one end to the other, food goes in, waste comes out. Vertebrates get a few extra organs that help them digest more complex food more efficiently, though. In the most general terms, the vertebrate digestive system goes like this:

- an intake tube (mouth and oesophagus);
- a stomach or series of stomach-like chambers where food is broken down both physically and chemically into small particles;

ANIMALS: DIGESTIVE SYSTEM

- a series of intestines where nutrients from the food are absorbed into the body, usually with the help of chemicals secreted by organs such as the liver, gallbladder and pancreas; and
- a waste tube where any undigested material is gathered together and expelled from the body.

Beyond this, it's hopefully not a shock to anyone that a creature's eating habits have a big impact on what its digestion system looks like.

Digesting plants is a very different business to digesting meat. Generally speaking, plants are harder to digest because they have cell walls, so herbivore guts are usually a lot longer than carnivores', and they usually have bigger stomachs. This is also an advantage, though, because the food stays in their body for a lot longer, meaning they can extract more nutrients from it and they get a slow, sustained release of energy, rather than a single quick hit—yet another reason why herbivores are better at stamina, and carnivores are better at speed. Because plants are harder to digest, though, herbivores rely on an active and complex system of gut bacteria to help them break down their food.

Carnivores, on the other hand, have highly acidic stomachs in order to break down meat and other animal matter as quickly as possible, and because their stomachs are so acidic, few bacteria can survive in there—one of the key reasons that carnivores are less likely to get sick from eating spoiled food.

ANIMALS: DIGESTIVE SYSTEM

Did You Know?

In about 2014, scientific research about the gut exploded into the cultural consciousness. As it transpired, the saying 'You are what you eat' bears out a lot more truth than we ever previously suspected. Contemporary research has demonstrated that the types of microbes (mostly bacteria and fungi) that live in our gut exert a significant influence on our health, diet, and even lifestyle. Gut biome changes have been linked to obesity, depression, and even autism.

Their stomachs can also shrink and stretch very easily, since carnivores often have long periods of 'starvation' punctuated by successful hunts, and have to be able to eat as much as they possibly can all at once to tide them over.

Carnivores also have much bigger livers than herbivores, because meat is high in amino acids and other proteins that can actually be damaging in large quantities. The extra-big livers help to filter out these excess amino acids.

As well as these basic principles, some creatures—particularly earthworms (the only invertebrates other than octopuses, squid and cuttlefish to have separate digestive and circulatory systems) and birds—have an organ called a gizzard in their digestive tract, located after the stomach. This is a muscular organ that contains sand and small pieces of gravel which help to physically break up their food in order to make it easier for the intestines to digest.

ANIMALS: DIGESTIVE SYSTEM

As well as the internal organs, a creature's teeth and jaw are influenced by what and how it eats. Herbivore jaws fit loosely together and can move from side to side as well as up and down, which, when combined with large, flat-topped molars, allow for extremely efficient grinding. They also have very strong jaw muscles to allow for their near-constant chewing.

On the other hand, carnivore jaws fit tightly together so they don't dislocate when gripping struggling prey. Their teeth are sharp and molars are pointed rather than flat topped; unlike herbivores, who grind their plant matter, the molars shear against each other like scissors to help tear up the animal flesh. Carnivores' canine teeth are especially prominent and are used for gripping and holding.

Did You Know?

The teeth of carnivorous fish are similar to those of terrestrial carnivores. However, herbivorous fish can't chew in the same manner as terrestrial herbivores, as the continuous movement would interfere with the flow of water over their gills and they would suffocate.

Instead, herbivorous fish generally have no teeth in their jaws, and instead have pharyngeal teeth, or teeth located way down in their throat (the pharynx).

So maybe think twice before sticking your finger down a fish's throat!

ANIMALS: DIGESTIVE SYSTEM

In contrast, the incisors (front teeth) are more important in herbivores, as they are used for cutting grass and other plant matter (although interestingly, some large herbivores such as cows and sheep have only lower incisors; in place of upper incisors they have a tough, gummy pad).

One final thing to consider on the topic of digestion: we've looked at what goes *in*, and what happens to it once it's there, but what about what comes *out*?

There are two key components to digestive waste: liquid waste and solid waste.

While mammals excrete solids and liquids separately, birds and lizards (and insects and land snails) don't. Their kidneys are differently developed and they don't produce water-soluble urea, instead producing uric acid that is excreted as a paste along with solid wastes (the uric acid is the white part of the familiar brown-and-white bird poo splash).

The reason for this is that their less-developed kidneys can't concentrate urine like mammals' kidneys can (which is why your urine gets darker when you're dehydrated), so if they excreted water-soluble urea, they would quickly become dehydrated. Excreting their 'liquid' waste mixed with solid waste as a paste allows the bird or reptile to hold onto extra water in their body.

Fish are a different story again: freshwater fishes excrete liquid waste almost continuously, producing an extremely dilute ammonia solution (which mostly

ANIMALS: DIGESTIVE SYSTEM

passes out through their gills)—as do amphibians when they're submerged.

Saltwater fishes also excrete extremely dilute ammonia through their gills, but only in very small amounts.

And while we're on the subject of waste, remember that it's only what goes in that comes out, and even then in a compacted form. Once again, a nod to the *Jurassic Park* film: those Triceratops droppings? *Way* too much for one creature to excrete.

Carnivores generally produce less waste overall from what they eat, but because they eat larger, less frequent meals, each individual set of droppings can be larger (comparative to the size of the animal).

Herbivores, on the other hand, produce a large amount of waste overall, and because they eat continuously they also tend to excrete relatively continuously. Some herbivores produce whopping great droppings (e.g. cows and other bovines), but it's more common for herbivores to have frequent, smaller excretion—including some species who simply drop 'pebbles' all day long (e.g. sheep, kangaroos, deer species).

In general terms, endotherms (previously called 'warm-blooded') create more waste than ectotherms (previously called 'cold-blooded') because they eat more to fuel their higher energy needs.

Which leads to the final issue: the where. In general, creatures who live in defined 'home' areas, such as burrows or nests, are more careful about

ANIMALS: DIGESTIVE SYSTEM

where they toilet. Usually this means to carnivores and omnivores, but obviously there are many herbivores who also keep 'clean' home areas.

Migrating herd animals, on the other hand, are unlikely to ever visit the exact same patch of grass twice, and so really couldn't care less about where they let fly.

Some people have suggested that this is why humans generally keep carnivores as pets: carnivores

> ### DID YOU KNOW?
>
> A dominant theory about the trainability of carnivores is that any creature that has to hunt for its food (or part thereof) has 'superior intelligence'. (Though this is difficult to quantify in any case because our definition of 'intelligence' is still so murky.)
>
> Pack coordination is certainly a component that helps create 'intelligence', but many (most) herbivores exist in herds, which can also be quite coordinated—so intelligence is not necessarily a function of being part of a large group so much as having the skills necessary to coordinate a hunt.
>
> There are exceptions to this still—rabbits can be trained to show jump, horses are obviously highly trainable—but as a very general trend, carnivores do tend to exhibit more of the traits that we would classically consider to be part of 'intelligence'.

ANIMALS: DIGESTIVE SYSTEM

usually have more fastidious manners when it comes to droppings and thus are more easily housetrained.

It's an interesting theory, but it's also worth noting that some herbivores can be successfully housetrained (rabbits, for example).

FOR EXAMPLE

Because my creature is a mammal and produces its own body heat, it's going to have a comparatively high metabolism, which means it's going to need comparatively more food than a similar-sized fish or reptile.

In the cold polar seas, plankton and krill flourish in spring and summer, and are virtually non-existent in autumn and winter. Fish that feed on the plankton and krill migrate in and out of the polar seas accordingly, providing food in a boom-or-bust cycle to creatures who live there.

This means that either my creature is going to need to be able to survive extended periods of little-to-no food, or it's going to have to migrate.

Migrating will bring it south into the seas right where I've concentrated my settlements, which makes for more potential human-animal clashes, so that's fabulous: we'll run with a migration pattern that follows the food.

Given I decided a couple of sections ago that the conflict this animal generates will stem from some sort of ability to interfere with sea transport, this means that winter and autumn are going to be slow trade periods for the populations in my little corner of the world, since their main shipping lanes will be clogged with these fancy, travel-disrupting creatures.

In order to get enough food to fuel its metabolism, my creature can either:
- be large but slow for its size, like a whale, and get its nutrients from plankton, krill, and sea vegetation, or
- be a speedy critter that zips through calories like an otter through water, and thus needs to eat meat for that fast hit of high-calorie energy.

Originally, I was thinking of something akin to a seal, but something the size of a sea otter could increase the conflict more: being smaller and more agile and speedier, the creature would be harder to trap, harder to contain, and more of them could live in a defined area, which means the havoc they wreak on shipping could be proportionately larger.

So, there's my decision at last: an otter- or penguin-sized sea mammal with flippers for its fore limbs and a seal-like tail for its hind limbs (clearly *not* an otter, you see, or even a penguin), a decent covering of blubber to insulate it against the cold seas, and a diet of fish—maybe with some shellfish thrown in there, although I'm not sure how one goes about opening molluscs when one has only flippers, so perhaps not after all!

Smallish fish, then.

Which means front-set eyes for depth perception, sharp teeth, large canines, a strong, close-fitting jaw, and the potential for bursts of intense speed—another thing that will make it harder to catch.

THE CIRCULATORY AND RESPIRATORY SYSTEMS: CIRCULATING NUTRIENTS

By now, between the skeleton, muscles, and need for hair or fat deposits, you should have a fair idea of what your creature looks like on the outside.

However, there is another factor that determines what your creature will look like, and that's the internal systems it has for circulating vital gases and nutrients around the body. (For most creatures, 'vital gases' means oxygen. However, some creatures use other gases instead—see *Did You Know?* on page 115.)

Small creatures can afford to have very simple systems, because the nutrients and gases don't need to travel far.

However, large creatures need increasingly complex systems the bigger they get, because nutrients and gases can't just diffuse through the body. Instead, complex organs like lungs and delivery systems like arteries and veins are needed to help transport these vital nutrients and gases.

INVERTEBRATES

Earthworms, squids, cuttlefish and octopuses have circulation systems that are more like the systems vertebrate creatures use. But other than these few creatures, invertebrates generally have two options for circulatory systems:

ANIMALS: CIRCULATION

- Creatures with hydrostatic skeletons tend to have 'gastrovascular cavities' in place of proper circulation systems.
- Creatures with exoskeletons tend to have open circulation systems.

Gastrovascular cavities are just a large cavity inside the creature that's directly connected to the outside—think sea anemones. These creatures don't have complex organs and are rarely more than a few millimetres thick in any place in their body to allow nutrients and gases to diffuse easily throughout their various body tissues.

This is clearest in sea creatures such as jellyfish: although they can grow very large (the Lion's Mane jellyfish can reach lengths comparable to a blue whale), they are full of cavities that allow the seawater to bathe most of their cells directly, and any internal cells they have are rarely more than a few millimetres away from the seawater.

Open circulation systems, on the other hand, are more common in creatures that have exoskeletons, such as insects. It's the next step up from gastrovascular cavities, and a step below having a genuine digestive and circulation systems.

Open circulation systems combine digestion and circulation into one simple system: the heart pumps a fluid called hemolymph around the creature's body, and the hemolymph carries nutrients and gases to all the creature's cells.

ANIMALS: CIRCULATION

Did You Know?

Blood is red because it contains haemoglobin, which is largely made up of iron. Haemoglobin binds oxygen so it can be easily transported around the circulatory system.

However, there are other options. Some octopods (octopuses, squids and cuttlefish), for example, have naturally blue blood. These octopods' circulatory systems (which are closed, like that of vertebrates) are based on haemocyanin instead of haemoglobin, which is copper-based rather than iron-based (Vulcans in the *Star Trek* series use copper in their blood too). It performs the same task of binding oxygen, but unlike haemoglobin, which gets so attached to its oxygen at low temperatures that the oxygen can't diffuse throughout the body, haemocyanin still works effectively as an oxygen diffuser even at below-zero body temperatures.

So, technically, you could create creatures that used an oxygen-binding mechanism other than iron-based haemoglobin, and their blood could be a colour other than red—and if your creatures regularly live in below-zero temperatures and can't regulate their own body temperature, you'll need to use something other than haemoglobin anyway.

(So next time a bug splatters on your windscreen, remember: bugs don't have blood! Even if it's disturbingly red, it's hemolymph!)

ANIMALS: CIRCULATION

These open circulation systems are handy because they require a lot less energy to run. However, they're also more vulnerable, because if you damage one system, you've damaged them all, and they have an in-built size limit. Like gastrovascular cavities, they rely on simple diffusion from the environment (insects don't breathe like we do; they just absorb oxygen from the air around them), so they're not very strong. This is yet another reason in addition to exoskeletons why you can't have giant bugs running around. In fact, the largest known insect to ever have lived on Earth was only about a foot long.

VERTEBRATES

Obviously, in order to grow bigger, creatures need a more complex circulation system.

A water flea has many more times the surface area relative to its mass than, for example, a blue whale does, and yet a blue whale is able to grow much, much larger. How does it manage this, and still get enough oxygen and nutrients out to every single one of its cells?

Simple: by increasing its internal surface area. Lungs are full of crevices and folds, with alveoli increasing the surface area even further; blood vessels split from arteries to veins and finally to tiny capillaries, which in the human body could be laid out end to end for a distance of 100,000km.

ANIMALS: CIRCULATION

Gills serve a similar function in fish, increasing the surface area and allowing them to absorb more oxygen from the surrounding water.

Because of this increased complexity, the delivery of gases and nutrients around the creature's body is much more efficient, so the creature can afford to grow bigger.

Eating habits affect the kind of circulation systems an animal has too. Generally speaking, the cardiovascular system of carnivores is designed to allow maximum efficiency for short periods of time; what this means practically is that carnivores can exert themselves heavily, running at incredible speeds and performing marvels of agility and strength, but only for shorter periods of time—the time needed to run down prey.

Conveniently, this matches with the way they consume their calories: in short, intense bursts. Meat is very high in calories and nutrients, which is another reason why carnivores can easily go a couple of days without a meal.

Did You Know?

Birds have a particularly strong cardiovascular system, with a heart that beats much more rapidly than that of land animals. Their lungs are small, but are kept permanently inflated, even when they are breathing out, to increase their ability to diffuse oxygen.

ANIMALS: CIRCULATION

Herbivores, on the other hand, have to be active for most of the day in order to eat enough plant matter to get all their calories. Instead of being built for speed, they're build for stamina, often having deeper, larger chests than the carnivores that live in their area, with large, highly efficient lungs.

Omnivores, on the other hand, are likely to be neither particularly massive, nor particularly powerful, nor built especially for speed. Instead, they are generalists, with a physical frame designed to accommodate a fairly average-sized, average-functioning cardiovascular system.

FOR EXAMPLE

Knowing now that my creature is a carnivore, I know that it's going to have a sleek and speedy sort of frame.

This is a bit relative, though, because it still needs to keep those blubber stores for warmth; a seal is a carnivore too, but it only looks sleek and speedy in the water. On land, they look pretty darn awkward!

So: we're looking at something kind of like a miniature seal, I think.

THE REPRODUCTIVE SYSTEM: MAKING MORE ANIMALS

There are two main ways that creatures go about making more of themselves: asexual and sexual reproduction. Asexual reproduction is when one creature creates genetically identical offspring from a part of itself. It's an advantage because the creature doesn't need anything else in order to create a new generation; reproduction is pretty much a given so long as the environment is right.

In contrast, sexual reproduction involves the fusion of an egg and sperm to create a new, genetically distinct creature. Because the new generation is genetically diverse, sexual reproduction is a huge advantage in environments that change frequently. If all the new generation had the same genes, one environ-mental change could kill them all. However, having offspring with lots of different genes means that generally, no matter how the environment changes, at least some of the new generation will survive.

Within these two general spheres, though, the ways animals have developed in order to create new animals are about as varied as you could imagine.

ANIMALS: REPRODUCTION
Did You Know?

One thing that isn't possible to plausibly imagine, however, is interbreeding between humans and aliens. If you're writing fantasy or science fantasy, then by all means, hand wave the biology away.

But if you're striving for hard science fiction, or something that's remotely plausible, you'll have to forego these mixed matings: horses and donkeys can't even interbreed without producing sterile offspring, and humans and apes can't produce viable offspring at all.

So, sadly, unless you go with the also-kind-of-hand-wavy method of gene splicing and complicated IVF (and even then you're assuming that your aliens use similar DNA to humans, a pretty vast assumption), human-alien children just ain't gonna happen.

(Alien parasites invading human bodies to use as hosts, on the other hand, is much more plausible, although you'd have to question why said alien parasites had evolved the ability to reproduce in the pretty specific environment of the human body if they didn't have an abundant supply of humans to invade previously—sorry *Alien!*)

ANIMALS: REPRODUCTION

INVERTEBRATES

Asexual reproduction is a great option for creatures that live in highly stable environments like the ocean—especially creatures who might never come into contact with another adult of their species.

Because of this, it's the reproduction method of choice for most aquatic invertebrates—particularly corals, hydras and jellyfish. Some, like jellyfish, can actually reproduce asexually *or* sexually, depending on the environment, or, in some species, on where they are in their life cycle.

There are three main types of asexual reproduction:

- Fission, which is where one parent individual splits itself into two or more 'children' of approximately equal size (for example, sea anemones).
- Budding, which is where new individuals form as growths on the parent and can either split off entirely, or remain connected, forming colonies (for example, corals).
- Fragmentation, where the parent individual breaks up its body (often by dropping limbs) and one or all of the pieces grow into a new adult (for example, sponges).

Some creatures (bees, ants and wasps in particular, but also some fish, some amphibians, and the occasional lizard) can also reproduce asexually by laying eggs. Unlike birds, whose eggs need to be

ANIMALS: REPRODUCTION

fertilised in order to develop into baby birds, these other creatures lay unfertilised eggs that hatch and grow into clones of their egg-laying parent. Most of these species can lay both fertilised and unfertilised eggs, and insects in particular use this to establish a gender balance: male drones come from unfertilised eggs, and females come from fertilised eggs.

DID YOU KNOW?

Fertilisation is the process of fusing two genetically different gametes (sexual cells) together to create a genetically new and distinct organism. In contrast, unfertilised eggs contain genetic material from only the mother. In many species, an unfertilised egg is unable to develop into a mature individual. However, some species have unfertilised eggs that are able to develop and hatch.

Many invertebrates, particularly the worms, most insects, and arachnids, do reproduce sexually.

However, this isn't always straightforward. Parasitic worms and burrowing creatures, for example, run into difficulties because they can go for long periods of time without ever seeing another adult, but their external environment isn't stable enough to support asexual reproduction.

To address this problem, each individual is both male and female—hermaphroditism. In a few rare cases, a hermaphrodite can fertilise themselves (still considered sexual reproduction since an egg and a

ANIMALS: REPRODUCTION

sperm with varied genetic material are involved), but usually the advantage of being a hermaphrodite is that you don't have to wait for an adult who is also the right sex to come along, you just need any adult, and both partners can walk away from the union pregnant.

VERTEBRATES

Most vertebrates reproduce sexually, but not all follow the typical pattern of one male and one female. Notably, many fish species display sequential hermaphroditism, which is where each individual changes sex throughout its life cycle.

Australian blue wrasses are all hatched female. As they develop, they form social groups, and the largest member of each group undergoes physical changes, becoming the male in a harem of females and acting as the group's defender.

In contrast, clownfish are hatched sexless. The largest fish will become the dominant female, while the second largest will become the breeding male, with the rest remaining sexless. As with blue wrasse, if the largest and most dominant fish (male for the wrasse, female for the clownfish) is removed, the next largest fish will undergo physical changes, changing sex in order to fill in the 'power vacuum', as it were.

And of course, there are also species that are hatched male and become female, such as some varieties of oyster.

ANIMALS: REPRODUCTION

There are two options for sexual reproduction: internal and external fertilisation.

External fertilisation, however, requires a liquid environment for the eggs and sperm to be ejected into, both so that the eggs don't dry out and so that the sperm can swim to meet the eggs. Obviously this is something more suited to aquatic creatures, and indeed the vast majority of aquatic and amphibious vertebrates (fish, frogs, etc.) use external fertilisation.

The biggest issue here is timing, because the sperm and eggs have to meet at the right time without being swept away from each other. Because of this, environmental factors such as day length or temperature can cue the release of eggs and sperm from an entire population at once (corals do this as well as reproducing asexually), and chemical triggers can lead an individual to release its eggs or sperm when it detects the presence of compatible eggs or sperm in its surroundings.

Internal fertilisation is obviously the reproductive method of choice for creatures who don't live in water. Timing is still important, as an egg still needs to be released at the right time to meet the sperm, but rather than external cues like daylight and temperature, the cues for internal fertilisation are usually changes in behaviour and/or the release of pheromones (tiny water-soluble or air-borne molecules that are extremely potent).

Creatures who practice internal fertilisation usu-

ANIMALS: REPRODUCTION

ally have much more complex reproductive systems, and in general are designed so that the egg and sperm meet up inside the female.

Generally speaking, creatures that fertilise externally will produce far more offspring than those that fertilise internally. This is to compensate for the fact that many eggs will go unfertilised altogether, and for the decreased levels of parental care.

Additionally, an animal's overall complexity also affects the number of young it will produce.

Complex young take a lot more energy to produce and raise, but are also more likely to survive, so fewer are needed—hence, the larger the animal, the fewer the young.

Did You Know?

The so called 'fourth trimester', a concept coined by Dr Harvey Karp (a US paediatrician born in the 1950s), suggests that human babies are born significantly less developed than other mammals, and that their first three months of life effectively represents a 'fourth trimester' in their development.

Essentially, the idea is that human babies should really be in the womb for a full year, but that they are born early due to the significant growth in brain/head size that occurs during their first three months post-birth; if they were to gestate for twelve months, their heads would not fit through the mother's birth canal.

ANIMALS: REPRODUCTION

Herbivores also produce a lot more young than carnivores, both because they have more available food and to compensate for the risk of losing babies to predators.

The final factor determining how many young a creature will produce is their brain development. Large, complex brains need longer periods of incubation, either in a protective egg or else inside the mother. This significantly reduces the number of pregnancies a mother can have in a year, and also the number of babies a mother can have at once.

(It's interesting to note, therefore, that humans don't actually have the longest pregnancies; that honour goes to the elephants, who are pregnant for about 21 months, and who also usually have only one baby.)

FOR EXAMPLE

Although the reproductive habits of my little critter aren't going to be a major feature of the story, it's still worth considering what I can do to increase the conflict potential.

My creature is a mammal, which means sexual reproduction, so there will be male creatures and female creatures.

The migratory pattern of my creature (north in summer, south in winter) means that it's going to be wanting to breed right as it's due to migrate north again. I can either have pregnant mothers stay behind and effectively starve for a while, as with whales, or I can borrow a trick from birds: penguins migrate back early and lay eggs, which means they're (comparatively) close to food, but their young are protected because while there are many aquatic predators in polar waters, there are very few on land.

So. My creature is going to be one of those funky mammals that lay eggs, and they'll breed up in the polar islands.

On the whole version of the map (see *How To Map*), these islands are near a 'mysterious blank section' that arose out of a mistake I made when sketching the maps (mapping mistakes are great fodder for worldbuilding).

This is a great opportunity to increase conflict,

because any intrepid explorers wanting to explore that mysterious blank section will need to head fairly close past these breeding islands. So, if my creatures get protective over their breeding grounds and/or their young, they'll try to hassle the explorers until they're out of the area—one way that they can easily interfere with transport.

I also want a way for them to interfere with transport apart from just hassling people during breeding season—to maximise conflict, they also need to be a pain when they're hanging out down south during winter, too.

Given that I want to write a fantasy world (because I usually do) with magically-powered vessels, the obviously solution is to give the creatures the ability to interfere with this magical source of power in some way—to slow it down or make it cut in and out unreliably.

This is *great*, because it means that any explorers near the breeding grounds may get stuck there for longer as their 'engines' play up, which means they get hassled more, which makes the engines harder to run... You see how this goes. Conflict! Hurrah!

Eggs would also be a valuable source of protein for explorers in those waters, and might even be enough of an enticement for them to risk transport failures to get the eggs. This means they'll be intruding even further into the creatures' territory, further increasing the conflict.

Excellent. Mission accomplished.

THE SENSES

While animals' senses differ widely across the animal kingdom, there are some basic types of input that scientists are pretty sure all animals can sense in at least one form or another:
- Mechanical input includes things like pressure, touch, motion, gravity and sound.
- Chemical input includes the obvious things like taste and smell, but also senses like pheromone detection and even thirst.
- Electromagnetic input includes visible light, infrared light, ultraviolet light, electricity and magnetism.
- Thermal input is simply heat and cold.

Finally, pain is fairly self-explanatory, but it can be divided further:
- heat-related pain
- pressure-related pain
- chemical-related pain (the kind that happens with inflammation, for example).

INVERTEBRATES

While senses such as taste or touch can vary widely across animals regardless of whether they are vertebrates or invertebrates, three senses that do differ markedly depending on whether or not the creature has a backbone are gravity, sound and sight.

ANIMALS: SENSES

(For a discussion on the other senses, see the 'vertebrate' section.)

Most invertebrates use little round chambers located in strategic positions around their body to detect **gravity**. These little chambers have a tiny particle in them, often similar to a grain of sand, and are lined with pressure sensors. The 'sand' grain falls according to gravity, setting off the sensors that it touches and thus telling the creature which way is down.

When it comes to **sound**, instead of the internal ears of most vertebrates, most insects have body hairs of different stiffnesses and lengths that vibrate at different frequencies (there haven't really been any investigations into how non-insect invertebrates detect sound). This means they can't hear a terribly wide *range* of sounds, but it also means that they're extremely sensitive to the range of sounds they *can* hear. A male mosquito, for example, can hear the wing beat of a female across a room.

The range of sound an insect's body hairs are tuned to can also be a defence mechanism: some caterpillars have body hairs that are tuned into the buzzing of predatory wasps.

As well as these sound-sensitive body hairs, many insects also have basic 'ears' located in their legs. These 'ears' are just a thin membrane stretched over an air-filled chamber, and they work like a simplified eardrum, with the membrane compressing the air in the chamber as sound waves hit it, which activates

ANIMALS: SENSES

pressure sensors in the chamber. Some moths use this system to hear the high-pitched sonar squeaks of the bats that prey on them, and cockroaches use it to detect when your foot is about to come crunching down on top of them.

As for **sight**, invertebrate eyes work on one of three models:

- Eyespots, used by very simple invertebrates such as flatworms.
- Single-lens eyes, used by some jellies, marine worms, spiders and many molluscs, as well as cephalopods (octopuses, cuttlefish, etc.).
- Compound eyes, used widely by insects and crustaceans, as well as some marine worms.

Eyespots are the simplest of all light-detecting organs, only sending information about light intensity and direction without any associated image. These types of organs are used by creatures who either don't have a lot of access to light, such as in the deep seas, or who only really need to be able to tell where the light is so they can get away from it, as in the case of flatworms, who dry out in light and warmth.

Single-lens eyes function pretty much the same way as a camera lens, with a small opening for the light to enter in and a layer of light-receptive cells at the back where the light focuses. Muscles around the eye can make the opening bigger or smaller and can change the focus of the light to see objects closer or

ANIMALS: SENSES

further away (this is different to vertebrate eyes, which focus by changing the shape of the lens).

Single-lens eyes can transmit an image to the brain, but it's blurrier and less distinct that images formed using either a compound eye or a vertebrate eye. However, creatures with a single lens can definitely see in colour, and some, like octopuses and squid, can even see polarised light—the same effect we get if we put on a pair of polarised sunglasses.

Single-lens eyes are also pretty good at detecting movement. These are the eyes of choice for invertebrates who need to see more than just where the light is, as with eyespots, but who don't need the extreme detail of compound eyes. Most marine invertebrates use single-lens eyes because they're not as finicky as compound eyes, which tend not to function as well in salt water.

Compound eyes, on the other hand, consist of up to several thousand individual light detectors, each measuring the intensity (and colour) of the incoming light. The image transmitted to the brain is a mosaic of individual pictures, so it's not very useful if you were wanting to, say, draw an accurate representtation of the landscape around you.

On the other hand, compound eyes are *excellent* at detecting movement; for comparison, humans can detect flashes up to about 50 times per second, while some insects with compound eyes can see the individual flickers of a light flashing at 330 times per second.

ANIMALS: SENSES

Put it this way: if these insects sat down to watch a movie, they'd be able to see every single individual frame.

Compound eyes are also fantastic at detecting colour. Human eyes detect three basic colours: green, red and blue. Dogs can only detect two: green and blue (no, they don't see black and white!). Some dragonflies, however, can see up to thirty different base colours (we can literally only imagine what this might look like), and bees can see ultraviolet (UV) light.

Compound eyes are almost exclusively used by insects. They need to be able to detect fast movements both in order to avoid predators and also because they themselves are very fast movers; if you're moving at a high speed relative to your body size and are twisting and turning a lot with agile movements, it's obviously an advantage to have an eye that detects movement super quickly and that doesn't need to take time to focus when the landscape changes.

Finally, a quick note on **chemical senses**: although most invertebrates don't have a dedicated 'nose' per se, they have receptors all over their body that can detect various chemicals and pheromones; these are particularly concentrated in their antennae.

Insects are especially sensitive to pheromones given out by potential mates, and sometimes even by the plants that they eat—sick plants attract insects much more quickly than healthy ones because the insects can detect chemically that the plant's immune system is compromised.

And on the topic of food, it seems logical that insects can **taste** with their mouths or mouthparts—but actually, many of them can taste through tiny hairs on their feet as well!

VERTEBRATES

MECHANICAL SENSES

Vertebrates pretty much all detect sound in the same way, although some systems (e.g. those of mammals) are a little more complex.

The basic principle, though, is that there is an inner chamber in the body—and internal ear—that may or may not open up externally (it mostly does, but fishes in particular lack ear holes), which is full of fluid and responds to sound vibrations by vibrating small bones. Fine hairs surrounding the fluid-filled chamber detect changes in pressure and transmit these signals to the brain, which interprets the results as sound.

These fluid-filled chambers are also useful because they double up as gravity sensors, functioning in much the same way as the little air pockets that invertebrates have.

Vertebrates can sense both the volume of sound—how strong the sound waves are—and the pitch of the sound—its frequency, or how fast the waves are oscillating, which we interpret as 'high' sounds if the

ANIMALS: SENSES

oscillation is faster and 'low' sounds if the oscillation is slower. There's a lot of variation as to which creatures can detect which range of frequencies. As animals go, humans can hear a pretty broad range of sounds (from about 20 to 20,000 Hertz, if that matters to you).

Fishes can hear about two-thirds that range of sounds, missing out on the very high and very low.

Birds can hear approximately the upper two-thirds of what humans can, but are much, much more sensitive to pitch and rhythm, being able to pick out an individual bird in a noisy flock.

LOGARITHMIC CHART OF THE
HEARING RANGES OF SOME ANIMALS

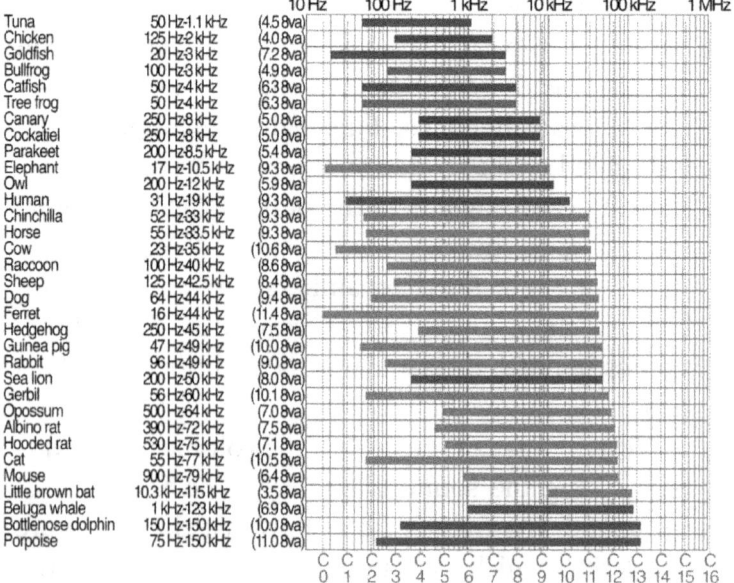

ANIMALS: SENSES

Frogs can hear about half of the human range (the middle half) and their ears are highly attuned to the pitch of each species' call.

Land mammals can generally hear a similarly wide range of sounds to humans, but starting and ending a bit higher on the sound spectrum (though notably, cows and ferrets can hear both higher and lower sounds than humans), and there's a slight tendency for smaller mammals to have a smaller range of hearing (missing out on low- to mid-range sounds, probably because their vocal cords are too small to produce such low sounds, so the low-range sounds don't matter—and also because communicating in frequencies too high for predators to hear is an advantage).

Marine mammals are similar to land mammals, but can often hear even higher-pitched sounds

Bats have a significantly smaller range of hearing than any of the above creatures, but can also hear higher into the spectrum than any others (although dolphins use this very high range as well).

One other vertebrate of note is the elephant, who can hear—as far as we know—the lowest notes of any vertebrate. Low-pitched sounds travel farther and more clearly than high notes, and studies have shown that elephants can transmit messages to each other over vast distances by stomping on the ground, which sends out a very low-pitched rumble in addition to the higher notes that we hear when they stomp.

ANIMALS: SENSES

> **DID YOU KNOW?**
>
> Hearing is an extremely important sense both for predator-carnivores, and for prey-herbivores. Predators need to be able to be extremely quiet to conceal their location, and prey herbivores need to be able to detect the slightest sound that might warn them of an incoming predator.
>
> Once again, dinosaur movies (and other movies that focus on how terrifying large predators are) lead us astray: if T-Rexes really did shake the ground as they ran, they'd never be able to get close enough to actually *capture* any prey, because they'd be heard coming from miles away!

The other mechanical input that vertebrates can sense is touch. Although for many years scientists assumed that the information conveyed by skin—our main touch-sensing organ—was limited to messages about pressure, vibrations, temperature, itches and pain, in the late 1990s researchers discovered that the slower nerves in our touch system, previously thought to just boost pain messages by conveying aches and throbs, actually respond best to slow, careful touches.

Further research confirmed it: these slow nerves are specially tuned to the kind of touch-pressure conveyed by activities such as grooming in monkeys,

ANIMALS: SENSES

licking in cats and dogs, and stroking, rubbing or massaging in humans. Why?

We know now that this kind of touch releases endorphins, but recent studies also suggest that this kind of touch actually strengthens social bonds in the brain, improving trust relationships and group co-operation. In fact, psychologists believe that this kind of touch-perception is probably critical to forming our individual identities.

Fish in particular are very sensitive to touch. Although they may not use stroking, licking or grooming to bond socially like mammals do, they have extremely sensitive receptors running in a line internally through the centre of their body, called the lateral line. These receptors, which are the shape of tiny, tiny hairs, are embedded in a jelly-like substance and function similarly to ears—in fact, in many fish there isn't much distinction at all between hearing sounds and sensing touch vibrations.

The vibrations these receptors detect give the fish information about current direction and strength (similar to how the hairs on our skin help us to detect wind direction and strength), and also about the location of nearby fish, allowing them both to stick together in schools, and to detect prey.

CHEMICAL SENSES

Vertebrates, like invertebrates, can sense a variety of things via chemical receptors in their body. Taste,

ANIMALS: SENSES

smell and pheromones are the most significant of these.

Taste is particularly important because, generally speaking, sweetness indicates easy-to-digest energy, bitterness can indicate poison, and sour tastes can sometimes be a helpful indicator that food has spoiled.

It's widely believed that animals taste the same tastes as humans—so sweet food tastes sweet, salty food tastes salty, and so forth. However, hunting carnivores have the least developed sense of taste, because it's less important for them to be able to distinguish between different food types: they only eat meat, and if they're hunting for most of it, it's unlikely to be spoiled.

Remember too that the stomach and gut of carnivores is much more acidic than omnivores or herbivores, so if they do eat a little food that is spoiled, the harmful bacteria is pretty much destroyed before it can do any damage—hence the observation that most dogs have "cast-iron" stomachs!

(Although, it must be said, technically canines are omnivores rather than true carnivores, which is why they can taste sweet flavours; felines, being true carnivores, can't taste sweet at all, and neither can dolphins or sea lions, both of which are also true carnivores.)

Herbivores, on the other hand, have the most developed sense of taste, and grazing herbivores like cattle or deer and their relatives have much, much

ANIMALS: SENSES

more sensitive tongues than humans. This is because it's vitally important that they be able to avoid poisonous plants—and because for some animals, especially animals from the savannah biome, it's how they identify the one type of grass they eat out of the hundreds of species around.

This is why you never keep horses to graze a paddock down; they're notoriously fussy about the types of grasses they will and won't eat. Cows or sheep, who, although they have extremely sensitive tongues, have a much broader palate, do a better job of keeping grasses (and weeds) uniformly cropped.

Omnivores such as humans sit somewhere in the middle. For comparison, humans have about 10,000 taste buds. Dogs have about 1,700, cats fewer than 500, pigs 14,000 and cows around 25,000.

Birds generally have even poorer senses of taste than cats, while reptiles—who both taste *and* smell with their tongues—can compete with most omnivores, even though they are often carnivorous.

In contrast, smell generally isn't as refined as taste, because it's harder to separate out different smells in air than it is in liquid or solid form.

There seems to be a rough correlation between excellent vision and a poorer sense of smell, and vice versa. Humans (and other primates) have fantastic vision, but aren't renowned for their ability to smell things at great distances.

On the other hand, mammals generally have the best senses of smell, with guinea pigs, dogs, horses,

ANIMALS: SENSES

mice, cows, opossums, rats and elephants all making the top ten of the World's Best Noses list (elephants are number one).

Frogs, and likely some turtles, also rank in the top ten, and reptiles generally can hold their own with their combined taste/smell sense.

Out of the mammals, the groups with the best sense of smell are the carnivores generally, but out of the herbivores, ungulates (which are hoofed animals, including horses, cattle, pigs, giraffes, camels, deer and hippopotamuses) have the best sense of smell. Carnivores have excellent scent perception because they have to sniff for prey, and ungulates do also because they are the most heavily preyed upon carnivores and have to keep watch for predators.

Birds, on the other hand, generally have pretty poor senses of smell. There are a few notable exceptions though: petrels and albatrosses are thought to be able to smell fish in the ocean while they are soaring up in the air. Some species of vultures can perform similar feats when scavenging for leftover meat, and kiwis, the little flightless natives of New Zealand, are also reputed to have an excellent sense of smell in their long, skinny beaks.

In the water, taste and smell are the same thing. Fish have very good senses of taste/smell, and although—like all other vertebrates—they have tongues with taste buds, they also have taste/smell sensors in their skin, especially down their lateral lines (a line running down each side).

ANIMALS: SENSES

Some, like catfish species, also have taste receptors in their whisker-appendages; in fact, catfish top the taste bud charts with more than 100,000 taste buds, mostly concentrated in their whiskers.

Interestingly, marine mammals such as whales and dolphins can't smell much at all in air, but have good senses of taste/smell in water.

ELECTROMAGNETIC SENSES

Fun fact: there's no discernible reason why vertebrates mostly rely on what we call 'visible light' (also known as white light), instead of on infrared and ultraviolet light. (Some theories suggest that it could be historically derived from the fact that white light is best at penetrating water—which means you can see through water best when you can see white light.)

While there are some obvious correlations between how a creature lives and what it can see, there is also a lot of randomness when it comes to sight as well. For example, many deep sea fishes can't see red light, because it doesn't penetrate deep into the ocean—but dogs can't detect red light either, even though there's lots of it around during the day.

Most fishes have some form of colour vision—but seals, whales, dolphins and the like can't see colour at all, receiving the world in black and white.

And despite the fact that some fishes can't see red, others can not only see red, but beyond red, into

ANIMALS: SENSES

infrared—typically piranha and other species that live in murky, poorly-lit waters. Some can even see polarised light.

Snakes can "see" infrared light; birds, jumping spiders, bees and butterflies can all see ultraviolet light, as can some species of shrimp; and sharks can't detect colour but can 'see' electrical radiation from their prey.

Short version? There are a whole lot of options when it comes to vision for vertebrates, and there enough exceptions to every rule that you can pretty much get away with anything.

There are some generally helpful principles though:

- Superior night vision (or low-light vision) usually comes at the cost of colour vision.
- Superior colour vision usually means poor vision in low lighting and often a lack of crystal-clear focus/depth perception.
- Black-and-white vision is better at detecting movement than colour vision.
- Creatures that hunt at night need better night vision.
- Creatures that hunt need better depth perception, which means eyes at the front of the head.
- Creatures that are hunted for prey need to be able to detect movement more than they need to see depth.

ANIMALS: SENSES

It's worth noting too that while colour vision is relatively common amongst fishes, amphibians, reptiles and birds, its relatively *un*common in mammals as a whole, despite being common in primates.

> ### DID YOU KNOW?
>
> Vision in general takes a lot of energy to maintain. This is one of the primary reasons why creatures that live in caves where they never see light don't have eyes: if vision isn't absolutely necessary, it's too 'expensive' to run.

As well as light radiation, some animals can sense electricity. Nearly all of these animals are fishes of some sort (including sharks, rays and eels), because water conducts electricity better than air. The only known exceptions are echidnas, some dolphins, cockroaches and bees.

There are two ways that animals can detect electrical activity: active and passive. Through the active method, they actively send out an electrical field and detect breaks or disruptions in the pattern. In the passive method, creatures detect the electrical impulses put out by all animals when nerves fire and muscles move.

Finally, some creatures can sense the magnetic field of the Earth, an ability that is closely tied to navigational ability. The exact mechanism by which they do this is still unclear, although in many cases it seems to be related to the iron-rich mineral magnetite, once used by sailors as a compass needle and found in the skulls of salmon, pigeons and sea turtles, in the abdomen of bees, and in the teeth of some molluscs.

It's long been theorised that some ability to detect the Earth's magnetic field is what enables birds and insects to successfully migrate across vast distances, but as noted, we're still not one hundred percent sure how.

This ability to detect magnetism seems to be common in birds, turtles, sharks and stingrays. It's also been found in mole-rats, some bats, foxes (who have a 75% better strike rate when catching mice if pouncing in a north-to-north-easterly direction compared to in any other direction), dogs (who apparently prefer to urinate with their body aligned north-south, all other factors being equal), and possibly in cattle and roe deer, who appear to prefer to graze with their body aligned north-south, although this evidence is a bit inconclusive.

FOR EXAMPLE

I still haven't figured out exactly what it is that allows my creature to interfere with shipping, and I think the time has come.

The most obvious route, to me, is that this is related in some way to the creature's ability to sense electromagnetic radiation.

In fact, a super-simple explanation is that the creature generates some kind of electromagnetic field at the same frequency or currency as the world's magical field (assuming that my magic is sourced from a field, which, let's just make that decision right now, it is!) that interferes with ships' movement mechanisms.

It's kind of playing off the idea of electric eels who generate an electric field and can tell where prey is by sensing disturbances in the field, and throwing in the idea of signal jamming (something that eels actually have a mechanism to avoid!).

So this means that if too many of the creatures come too near the propulsion system of the ship, the propulsion system gets jammed and stops working. I can see anti-signal-jamming research becoming a popular field of magical study!

So there we have it: my newly invented creature. Something like a miniature seal or sea lion, sleek and fast with front-facing eyes, sharp teeth, with two front flippers and a tail; a creature that chases down fish for prey, that migrates to the poles during the warmer seasons to feast and breed, and that, even though it's a mammal, lays eggs.

Also it's territorial over its breeding grounds, which means the males will probably fight for territory in the spring—and maybe that's another reason why these creatures are so bad for shipping: if the creatures can detect variances in the magical field, a ship would probably sound like a giant, incoming male that needs to be fought away.

One fancy new magical creature, designed specifically to increase conflict in my story. Done.

PART THREE
TINY LIFE: NEITHER PLANT NOR ANIMAL

You're probably not going to need to create your own tiny life for your story, unless it revolves around some new kind of plague. However, in the interests of being complete, we're going to conclude with a brief look at the five main types of things-that-are-alive-but-aren't-plant-or-animals.

The category that people are most familiar with is fungi, a category of living things that for most of history was incorrectly included in the plant kingdom. Actually, fungi have more in common with insects than plants, but really they are neither plant nor animal.

The other familiar categories are viruses and bacteria, which we all know about because of their ability to cause illness.

Archaea and Protista are the two lesser-known categories, though many people will have looked at least briefly at some of these creatures in high-school science classes.

We'll examine each of the categories now in alphabetical order.

ARCHAEA

Plant cells have walls made out of cellulose, and animal cells, particularly insects, have chitin. In contrast, the cell walls of living things in the Archaea category are made from sugars and proteins.

Archaea don't really interact with humans in any direct way and they're all single-celled organisms, so our awareness of them is usually minimal.

However, they play a vitally important role in recycling nutrients. Archaea are so small that they break molecules down into smaller molecules, or even into individual atoms, which means that these atoms or smaller molecules can be recycled into new chemical compounds.

Plants and animals can build molecules, but can't break them down as efficiently as Archaea, so if there were no Archaea around, all plants and animals would eventually run out of these tiny building blocks and wouldn't be able to make the compounds they need to stay alive.

Archaea are able to reproduce very quickly, since they reproduce asexually by one cell splitting into two, dividing on average every 1 to 3 hours. They're also able to adapt to new environments very easily because 'adults' can swap DNA with each other. This adaptability means they can thrive in harsh environments where nothing else can live.

Archaea that live in really extreme environments are called extremophiles. Examples include:

TINY LIFE: ARCHAEA

- various species which thrive in extreme heat, some living in temperatures as high as 113C/235F in deep-sea hydrothermal vents;
- species which live in highly saline environments such as the Dead Sea;
- species that get energy anaerobically (i.e. without oxygen), in some cases actually being poisoned by oxygen; and
- some species that can endure extreme cold without shutting down.

DID YOU KNOW?

Symbiosis is an interaction between two organisms that benefits both, such as the relationship between tickbirds and cattle. The birds perch on the cattle and eat unsuspecting ticks: the birds get food, the cattle stay healthy.

However, in symbiotic relationships at the 'tiny life' level, the two organisms are often impossible to separate. One such relationship is between a species of sulphur-consuming bacteria and a species of methane-consuming Archaea, which combine together to form a ball-shaped mass. The bacteria feeds on the sulphurous waste products that the Archaea produces, and in turn increases the ability of the Achaea to metabolise methane.

These symbiotic bacteria-Archaea balls are found in ocean floor mud and consume around 300 billion kilograms of methane every year.

TINY LIFE: ARCHAEA

Extremophiles are often studied by astrobiologists exploring possibilities for life beyond Earth, and are a useful source of ideas for science fiction authors seeking to create alien life or creatures that can survive without oxygen.

Did You Know?

Some tiny life can stay frozen for decades, and even centuries, before thawing out to full life once again. One such example is anthrax, which is known to spend years at a time in cold soil, only to suddenly—and sometimes—mysteriously springing back to life again. This happened in 2016, when a herd of reindeer which had died of anthrax thawed in the permafrost, causing a fresh outbreak of the disease.

However, trendy though it may be to imagine all sorts of frozen plagues just waiting to be thawed in the permafrost, the reality is more complicated. Most tiny life that is pathogenic to humans needs the warm, wet environment of the human body in order to both survive and reproduce. Efforts at reviving frozen small pox, influenza and pneumonia have all failed (thank goodness, really).

So if you're wanting to play with this idea, you'll need to create a tiny lifeform specifically to withstand life outside the human body, as well as a way for it to impact human health.

BACTERIA

Like Archaea, most bacteria are single cells with walls made from modified sugars. There are many different categories of bacteria, but two are particularly important: gram-positive and gram-negative bacteria.

The difference between them has to do with their cell walls. Both are made out of modified sugars, as aforementioned, but gram-negative bacteria also have an outer membrane made out of carbohydrates and fats. While the exact chemicals that make up this outer membrane are different for each species of bacteria, they are usually toxic to humans and/or animals.

In contrast, gram-positive bacteria are usually pretty innocuous.

Bacteria can cause illness or disease usually by producing a poison, which can be either an exotoxin or an endotoxin.

Exotoxins are proteins that the bacteria actually secrete that have a negative effect on larger life forms; cholera and botulism are two examples.

Endotoxins are the toxic outer membrane of gram-negative bacteria. Because these toxins are part of the bacteria and aren't actually secreted, the bacteria can live happily inside a host organism with no ill effects; however, when the bacteria die and their cell walls decompose, the toxins in the wall are released, making the host sick. Nearly all species of

TINY LIFE: BACTERIA

Salmonella are endotoxic, from the varieties that cause food poisoning through to *Salmonella typhi*, which causes typhoid fever.

Another interesting group of bacteria are cyanobacteria, also known as blue-green algae, even though they are not an algae at all. Cyanobacteria are often considered to be the most self-sufficient of all organisms due to their unparalleled ability to 'fix' (acquire) nitrogen from the air.

All life requires nitrogen in order to make amino and nucleic acids (integral components of cells), but plants and animals are limited in the forms of nitrogen that they can use. In contrast, small life like bacteria can metabolise nitrogen from a very wide variety of sources, and none more efficiently than cyanobacteria.

Cyanobacteria are also noteworthy because they are the only prokaryotes (simple-celled organisms, unlike plants, animals, fungi and Protista) with the ability to photosynthesise, creating oxygen as a waste product when exposed to sunlight and carbon dioxide.

Cyanobacteria generally prefer a wet environment, and are abundant in both fresh and saltwater systems. Some species clump together to create bacterial colonies, and provide an important food source that underpins the entire aquatic food chain.

When too many of them clump together, however, they create an infestation that is commonly called a bloom of blue-green algae. In these concen-

TINY LIFE: BACTERIA

trations, cyanobacteria can cause diarrhoea, nausea, vomiting, skin irritations and breathing difficulties in humans.

Did You Know?

As a general rule, the types of hosts that are affected by a particular strand of bacteria are limited. Ants aren't really at risk from E. Coli, and the kinds of bacteria that infect plants aren't generally an issue for humans.

This is something you need to consider, though, if you're writing science fiction (or fantasy) that involves world-hopping: On the one hand, it's extremely unlikely that bacterial infections that affect humans would also kill off aliens who were utterly inhuman (why hello there, *War of the Worlds*—though H.G. Wells gets a bit of a free pass since germ theory wasn't well established when he was writing).

But on the other hand, it's also relatively plausible that if we ever did come across a planet that had life on it, some of the microorganisms would be dangerous, possibly even fatal—just not necessarily the ones that were considered an annoyance to the locals. Imagine, for example, aliens dying of the common cold, or lactobacillus, the family of helpful bacteria found commonly in yogurt.

FUNGI

This is the section on small life, and yet most of the fungi we are familiar with are much, much larger than a single cell. However, they fit into the 'Tiny Life' section because there *are* species that are microscopic, and more importantly, fungi are neither plant nor animal.

For a long time fungi were thought to be part of the plant kingdom, but evidence from the last 50 years clearly shows that fungi are actually more closely related to animals. Their cells walls are made of chitin, like the exoskeletons of insects, rather than cellulose, like the cell walls of plants, and they can't create their own food, as plants do, but must digest external forms of energy, like animals. In overly simple terms, you might say that fungi are brainless insects with an external digestive system.

Although single-celled fungi exist (these are called yeasts), most fungi are multi-celled. They typically form a network of fine tubes called hyphae, which are intriguing because although they consist of multiple cells, they share a single cell wall.

Like lungs and veins in complex animals, mycelium (the term for a large, dense mass of hyphae) grow into a dense and complicated network of fine endings in order to increase their surface area. Lungs do this so they can absorb as much oxygen from air as possible; veins maximise their surface area so they can transport blood directly to as many cells as possible. Mycelium are the fungus's digestive system and grow this way so they can absorb as many nutrients from their surroundings as possible. In fact, a single cubic centimetre of good quality organic soil containing mycelium can have as much as a kilometre of hyphae.

Fungi can be categorised according to what they feed on, much like animals:

- Saprobes, or decomposers, break down and absorb nutrients from nonliving organic material.
- Parasites absorb nutrients from living hosts (a bad thing for the host).
- Symbionts absorb nutrients from a live host, but in a way that is beneficial to the host, usually because the fungi also give nutrients back to the host.

Parasitic and symbiotic fungi often have specialised hyphae that can penetrate the cell walls of their hosts, and some can even react in order to trap food—for example, *Arthrobotrys*, a soil fungus, which sets traps for nematodes by forming hoops in its hyphae that constrict around the tiny worms when they wriggle through.

Fungi that form a symbiotic (mutually-beneficial) relationship with plant roots are called mycorrhizal fungi. This relationship is highly beneficial to the plants because the fungi break down the nutrients in the soil so that the plant can absorb them much more effectively. The mycorrhizal fungi even break down nutrients in the soil that the plant needs, but that the plant would never be able to access alone—phosphate ions, for example—making this relationship not just beneficial, but necessary.

Some fungi also form symbiotic relationships with animals, helping break down food matter in the stomachs of various mammals, particularly herbivores.

> DID YOU KNOW?
>
> Some species of ants and termites are known to 'farm' fungi, bringing the fungi cultures leaves and organic matter to feed on, which the fungi then break down into substances the ants can digest. The fungi functions as the stomach and digestive tract, while the ants provide the brain and limbs, and together they function as a single living organism.

Finally, fungi can form symbiotic relationships with other non-plant, non-animals. Most notably, fungi and algae can coexist symbiotically, and we call the resulting organism 'lichen'.

In lichen, the algae provide carbon compounds through their photosynthesis, and some varieties fix nitrogen out of the atmosphere. The fungi provide a safe and stable environment for the algae to flourish, catching water and minerals on which the algae can also feed.

TINY LIFE: FUNGI

Interestingly, lichen can function as a sort of air quality meter; because the vast majority of their nutrients are absorbed passively from the air and from rainwater, they are particularly sensitive to pollution, and mass die-offs can be one of the first signs of deteriorating air quality.

Fungi are extremely important to sustaining complex life. Not only do they break down organic matter and help to recycle nutrients, they also provide a food source, and many species have medical value—penicillin, a refined form of the mould *Penicillium* that grows on oranges, is perhaps the best-known antibiotic to come from fungi. Single-celled fungi, or yeasts, have long been used in baking and brewing, and mycorrhizae too are vital to human survival and development, boosting the productivity of food plants.

However, fungi are not all good: not only is their ability to speed up decomposition sometimes a bad thing (more English ships were lost to mould and rot than to enemy fire in the American War of Independence), they can sometimes cause illness.

Did You Know?

More than 40,000 people were killed in 944 A.D. in France, for example, because the rye supply was infected with ergots—the fungi that produces lysergic acid, the raw material for the hallucinogen LSD.

TINY LIFE: FUNGI

DID YOU KNOW?

> Fairy rings are often considered signs of fantastical activity, but in reality their formation is quite simple and logical. As a fungus grows underground, its 'roots' (hyphae) extend outwards in all directions equally if there is nothing to block their path. In many species, the above ground structures we call mushrooms are formed at the ends of these 'roots'. So if a single fungus is able to grow large enough and has a clear path, it will grow naturally into a roughly circular form, with mushrooms popping up around its circumference.

Most pathogenic (illness-causing) fungi are parasitic and affect plants; between 10 and 50% of the world's fruit harvest each year is lost to fungal infections.

Far fewer fungi cause illness in humans. Only about 50 species are known to be parasitic to humans and animals, including ringworm, athlete's foot, and other skin infections.

More dangerous are the systemic mycoses, fungal infections that spread throughout the whole body, usually by inhaled spores rather than parasitic hyphae.

Additionally, many fungi that usually coexist peaceably with humans and animals may become pathogenic if the body conditions change and become unusually favourable, allowing the fungi species to out-compete other necessary microbes.

TINY LIFE: FUNGI

Candida albicans, a yeast species, is a common example of a yeast that usually hangs out quite happily in the human body, but which can cause illness if it overgrows (usually when too many of the body's natural bacteria are killed off).

PROTISTA (INCLUDING ALGAE)

Protista, or protists, vary widely in their structure, modes of digestion, and function; in fact, research in the early 2000s suggests that protists vary so wildly in their characteristics that they are not actually one unified group at all, but a series of unrelated groups that only have in common the fact that they aren't anything else.

But generally speaking, protists live in liquid—and given they are mostly single-cellular, it doesn't have to be a lot of liquid at all. Hundreds of thousands of them can live in just a single drop of pond water.

There are somewhere between 65,000 and 200,000 protists in existence—a large but also finite and relatively comprehensible number.

- Some of them are fungus-like, absorbing nutrients passively from their surroundings.
- A large proportion are animal-like. Called *protozoa*, these animal-like protists propel themselves along with tiny, whip-like flagella that they wriggle like little spindly legs.
- The remaining portion are plant-like, because they can photosynthesise like plants. These plant-like protists we call *algae*, and although most protists are single celled, algae can grow extremely large—and then we call them sea weeds and kelps.

TINY LIFE: PROTISTA

There are four types of algae: golden, brown, red and green. Golden algae are tiny, usually just a single cell, and have a pair of flagella attached to one end of their cell. They're golden because they contain carotenoids, the same beneficial compound that gives carrots and sweet potatoes their orange colour, and the compound used by many creatures (including humans) to create vitamin A. Both fresh and saltwater plankton consists mostly of golden algae.

Brown algae are much larger organisms that can grow to spectacular lengths; in fact, the largest of all seaweeds and kelps belong to the brown algae family. Brown seaweeds are the algae most commonly eaten by humans.

Did You Know?

Many types of plankton have a special glow-in-the-dark feature called bioluminescence.

When disturbed, these tiny organisms emit chemicals that glow in an effort to warn predators away and even attract bigger predators to eat whatever is disturbing them.

Some fungi, some bacteria, and wide range of sea creatures (both vertebrates and invertebrates) also use bioluminescence, as do some insects on land, such as fireflies and glow worms.

Red and green algae are more closely related to plants than they are to golden and brown algae, but they have similar enough life cycles that they are all

TINY LIFE: PROTISTA

DID YOU KNOW?

> Diatoms are a family of single-celled algae (containing about 100,000 species) whose walls are particularly, and spectacularly, strong—so strong in fact that they can withstand pressure equivalent to one leg of a table that an elephant is standing on.
>
> Even more incredibly, they build these super-strong walls themselves, each diatom assembling microscopic building blocks to create its wall. Studies are under way to try to figure out exactly how diatoms do this; scientists hope to use the process as a model for nanotechnology, with plans to build teeny tiny motors, lasers, and medicine delivery systems.

still classified as algae. Red algae thrive in shallow waters, but because of their colour they can also live at much deeper depths than other algae because they are more efficient at harvesting sunlight. Despite their name, they are often greeny-coloured in shallow water, bright red in moderately deep water, and nearly black as the deepest end of their habitat.

Green algae, unlike the others, are mostly found in freshwater, though there are saltwater varieties. They are the most similar to plants (they have very similar cells and the way they harvest energy is almost the same), and range all the way from single-celled organisms with flagella to large sea lettuces. There are also some special species of green algae

TINY LIFE: PROTISTA

that can live out of water, something no other algae can do. These species live in a symbiotic relationship with fungi, and together they make lichens.

As well as all the varieties of protists that are harmless or even helpful to humans, there are also a large selection that can cause illness and disease. Unlike bacteria, this isn't always because the protists are toxic. Some are, but many are also parasitic.

Parasitic protists can reproduce by themselves by splitting one cell into two, but they need other creatures' cells to help them complete their life cycle. They invade and hijack these cells and the host creature then gets sick.

The protists behind malaria, sleeping sickness, toxoplasmosis and even potato blight function like this, reproducing asexually (by splitting one cell into two) until they are find their ideal host, where they then use specific cells to help them complete their life cycle. Malaria and sleeping sickness both hijack human red blood cells; toxoplasmosis uses the intestinal cells of cats; and potato blight invades various cells in the potato plant for this purpose.

Did You Know?

Blue-green algae aren't algae at all, but are actually colonies of cyanobacteria, photosynthetic bacteria that photosynthesise sunlight into energy just like plants.

VIRUSES

Viruses are a commonly known disease-causing agent (a pathogen). However, strictly speaking they're not alive. Far simpler than even the simplest cell, viruses are little more than DNA (or RNA) wrapped up in a protein shell. By themselves they can't reproduce or digest energy, and they're so small that millions could fit on a pinhead. A bacterium cell is about ten times smaller than an animal cell; a virus is ten times smaller again.

Instead of digesting and reproducing on their own, viruses work by invading host cells, locking onto receptors on the outside of the cell and injecting their DNA (or RNA) into it. This DNA (or RNA) is replicated by the enzymes in the host cell that would usually replicate the cell's own DNA, and together with new proteins that are also produced in the host cell, combine to create more virus particles, which are then expelled from the cell and go wandering off to find new cells to infect.

This process damages or completely destroys the host cell, which, along with the body's resulting immune reaction to having cells destroyed, is what causes the symptoms of viral infection.

Some viruses can also cause the host cell to produce toxins, and others have components, usually in their protein shell, that are toxic. And even cells that can repair themselves after infection by a virus can be affected long-term, as the virus may have caused or introduced mutations in the cell's own DNA. (Also, somewhat intriguingly, fragments of the virus itself can be left behind in the cell to be passed on when it reproduces, creating an interesting way for scientists to trace disease history.)

The types of cells infected by each virus are very specific because each type of virus fits into a particular shaped receptor, like a lock into a key.

For example, cold viruses infect the cells lining the upper respiratory tract of humans, while the AIDS virus infects certain types of white blood cells.

In contrast to these very specific viruses though, some viruses can infect a wide range of cells because their shape fits a wide variety of receptors: equine encephalitis virus, for example, can infect mosquetoes, birds, horses and humans.

The type of cell the virus infects also affects how easy it is to recover; colds are relatively easy to overcome because the cells in the human respiratory tract are good at repairing themselves.

Nerve cells, on the other hand, don't divide to create new nerve cells and they don't repair them-

DID YOU KNOW?

Also worth noting is the length of time it takes to come up with these vaccines. Check out the 2014/15 Ebola crisis: politics aside, you still can't create a fully-functional vaccine overnight, contrary to what *Outbreak* and *Independence Day* would have you believe.

selves efficiently, so the damage done by the poliovirus is permanent.

To prevent this kind of permanent damage, scientists have developed vaccines for some viral infections, which work by giving the body miniscule doses of the virus so that it can learn to recognise the virus as an intruder and kill it off. However, vaccines are not possible for all viruses, and whereas antibiotics can be used to cure bacterial infections because they stop the bacterial cells from working normally, viruses are not cells, and there are very few known drugs that can have any effect on viruses whatsoever.

FOR EXAMPLE

For my 'tiny life' example, I'm going to create a protist. In the interests of maximising conflict, it will of course be a parasite that can infect my people, and in order to maximally complicate things for them, it's going to be a waterborne parasite that lives in the ocean.

In real life, there aren't any algae that are parasites, but I'm imagining something like plankton, which is mostly golden algae. And since plankton is only 'mostly' golden algae, excellent: the protist I'm creating can be something found in the other bit of plankton, something which probably exists in a symbiotic relationship with golden algae—which means that my sea-faring travellers will have to be very wary of golden algae, because they won't know without testing it whether it's carrying my parasite or not.

And because parasites are gloriously flexible that way, my seafarers could pick it up from swimming in infected waters, or by consuming something that has the parasite in it.

So, waves glowing with phosphorescent plankton may look pretty, but people beware: the glow might just be sickly.

CONCLUSION

So, there you have it: the multitude of ways in which a plant or animal's environment and behaveiours will shape the way it looks.

Now when you set out to populate your invented worlds with beasts strange and fantastical, you can rest assured that they will be plausible and add conflict to your stories in ways you might never have imaged. Congratulations! You're practically a biologist, or a botanist, or both and you almost certainly won't use your newfound knowledge to cause chaos and destruction in the world!

Of course, there's always more to learn. It's not just plants and animals that are impacted by their environment—people are too! Watch out for *How To Create Cultures* (another *Inkprint Writers* title) to learn about all the myriad ways in which human cultures develop in response to their environments. It's not only obvious things like food and clothing that are affected—marriage practices, economic development and technological development are all impacted as well. Culture isn't just a grab-bag of pick-and-mix items; it's a complicated system of adaptations—so grab your copy of *How To Create Cultures* anywhere books are sold online to find out how it all works.

Then, of course, there are all the ways in which your planet's landforms influence its weather, and how its weather patterns then determine its biomes!

CONCLUSION

If you'd like to learn how to create your own maps with accuracy and aplomb, then watch out for *How To Map* (*Inkprint Writers #5*), a comprehensive and easy-to-follow guide to creating a gorgeous, plausible world for your populations to live in—and how to figure out where the different biomes are in the first place!

Thanks for joining me on this journey. I'd love to hear from you about your own experiences creating different creatures and plants.

I'm easy to find; you're most likely to get a response via @ByAmyLaurens on Twitter or Instagram, but you can also hunt me down at my website, www.amylaurens.com.

I hope to see you around!

ABOUT THE AUTHOR

ALTHOUGH AMY LAURENS is known for her expertise in the humanities, she studied biology and chemistry as part of her Masters program at the Australian National University, specialising in wildlife biology and environmental chemistry.

Amy has also published numerous other books, including the *Sanctuary* series of portal fantasy novels for children and the *Kaditeos* series of satirical fantasy for adults, some more non-fiction for writers (including the popular *How To Theme*), some non-fiction for people who are alive (mostly about dogs and parties, though not parties *with* dogs (yet?)), and a bunch of short stories in the *Inklet* collectible series.

You can find all Amy's books at:
www.amylaurens.com/books

INKPRINT WRITERS

Watch out for these other titles in the
Inkprint Writers series!

*How To Write Dogs: The 33 Worst Mistakes
Writers Make When They Write About Dogs*

How To Theme: Understanding and Analysing the Connection Between Theme and Story for Writers and Students

How To Create Cultures: How Climate Influences The Cultures You Create, A Reference For Writers, Gamers And Amateur Geographers!

How To Map: Be Accurate And Add Conflict To Your Story, A Reference For Writers, Gamers And Amateur Geographers!

FREE EBOOK

Thank you for buying this book!

When you buy an Inkprint Press book in print, we like to thank you by offering you the ebook for free. Please head to:

<http://www.inkprintpress.com/amy-laurens/how-to-create-life/>

and use the coupon LIFE100 to download your free copy in both .mobi and .epub formats. (The coupon will only work once.)

REFERENCES

PART ONE: PLANTS

Anders, Charlie Jane, and Jackson, Gordon. (2011.) "How To Create A Scientifically Plausible Alien Life Form." *Io9*. http://io9.com/5784971/how-to-create-a-scientifically-plausible-alien-life-form.

Biology Online. (2005.) *Bryophytes*. http://www.biology-online.org/11/12_bryophytes.htm.

Blum, A. (1996.) "Crop responses to drought and the interpretation of adaptation." *Plant Regrowth Regulation* 20:135-48.

Caldwell, Roy; Collins, Allen; Johnson Collins, Jennifer; et. al. (1996.) "The World's Biomes." *University Of California Museum Of Paleontology*. http://www.ucmp.berkeley.edu/exhibits/biomes/

Glover, B.J. (2009.) "The Diversity of Flower Colour: How and Why?" *International Journal of Design & Nature and Ecodynamics* 4(3):211-8.

Meyers, Noel, Campbell, Neil A. and Reece, Jane B. (2005.) *Biology 7th Edition: Australian Version*. Pearson Education, Australia.

Reekie, Edward, and Bazzazz, Fakhri A. (Eds.) (2011.) *Reproductive Allocation In Plants*. Academic Press, USA.

Science Theatre at Michigan State University. (1996.) "Why Are Plants Green?" http://www.pa.msu.edu/sciencet/ask_st/081496.html.

SolStation. (2011.) *Plants Under Alien Suns*.

http://www.solstation.com/life/a-plants.htm.

Thorne, R.F. (1992.) "Classification And Geography Of The Flowering Plants." *The Botanical Review* 58: 225-348.

Weiss, Martha R. (1995.) "Floral Color Change: A Widespread Functional Convergence." *American Journal of Botany* 82(2):167-85. DOI: 10.2307/2445525

Yong, Ed. (2014). "The Most Versatile Impressionist In The Forest." *Phenomena.* http://phenomena.nationalgeographic.com/2014/04/24/the-most-versatile-impressionist-in-the-forest/

PART TWO: ANIMALS

Albert, J. S. and Crampton, W. G. (2006.) "Electroreception and Electrogenesis." In Lutz, P. L. *The Physiology of Fishes.* Boca Raton, FL: CRC Press. pp. 429–470.

Angilletta Jr., Michael J., Steury, Todd D., and Sears, Michael W. (2004.) "Temperature, Growth Rate, and Body Size in Ectotherms: Fitting Pieces of Life-History Puzzle." *Integrative and Comparative Biology* 44 (6):498-509. DOI: 10.1093/icb/44.6.498

Bleckmann, H, and Zelick, R. (2009.) "Lateral line system of fish." *Integrative Zoology* 4:13-25. doi:10.1111/j.1749-4877.2008.00131.x

Brahic, Catherine. (2015.) "Dragonfly eyes see the world in ultra-multicolour." *NewScientist* 3010:19.

Brougher, Sam. (2012.) "The problem with giant exoskeletons." *Forest Azuaron.* https://forestazuarondotcom.wordpress.com/2012/06/18/the-problem-with-giant-exoskeletons/

Brougher, Sam. (2012.) "How to make plausible giant creatures." *Forest Azuaron.* https://forestazuarondotcom.wordpress.com/2012/06/13/plausible-giant-creatures/

Burda, H., Begalla, S., Červený, J., Neefa, J. and Němecd, P. (2009.) "Extremely low-frequency electromagnetic fields disrupt magnetic alignment of ruminants." *Proceedings of the National Academy of Science USA* 106: 5708–5713. doi:10.1073/pnas.0811194106

Cameron, James (dir.) (2009.) *Avatar.* Lightstorm Entertainment, USA.

Card, Orson Scott. (1992.) *Ender's Game.* Tor, New York.

Coplin, S. P. and Whitehead, D. (2004.) "The functional roles of passive electroreception in non-electric fishes." *Animal Biology* 54(1):1–25. doi:10.1163/157075604323010024

Duane, Diane. (1989.) *Spock's World.* Pocket Books, USA.

Fay, R.R. 1988. *Hearing in Vertebrates: a Psychophysics Databook.* Hill-Fay Associates, Winnetka IL.

Fay, R.R. and Popper, A.N. (eds.) (1994.)

Comparative Hearing: Mammals. Springer Handbook of Auditory Research Series. Springer-Verlag, NY.

Geddes, Linda. (2015.) "The Touch That Made You." *NewScientist* 3010:35-7.

Gould, S.E. (2012.) "Shine On You Crazy Diamond: Why Humans Are Carbon-Based Lifeforms." *Scientific American.* http://blogs.scientificamerican.com/lab-rat/2012/11/11/shine-on-you-crazy-diamond-why-humans-are-carbon-based-lifeforms/

Haldane, J.B.S. (2012.) "On Being The Right Size." *Physlink.Com: Physics & Astronomy Online.* http://www.physlink.com/Education/essay_haldane.cfm.

Hart, Vlastimil; Nováková, Petra; Malkemper, Erich Pascal; et. al. (2013.) "Dogs are sensitive to small variations of the Earth's magnetic field." *Frontiers in Zoology.* doi:10.1186/1742-9994-10-80

Heffner, H.E. (1983.) "Hearing in large and small dogs: Absolute thresholds and size of the tympanic membrane." *Behavioral Neuroscience* 97:310-318.

Hemsley, Susan. (2010.) "Do Animals Taste The Same Things As Humans?" *ABC Science.* http://www.abc.net.au/science/articles/2010/08/12/2980854.htm

Holland, R.A., Thorup, K., Vonhof, M.J., Cochran, W.W. and Wikelski, M. (2006.) "Bat orientation using Earth's magnetic field." *Nature* 444(7120):702.

Jakinovich, William and Sugarman, Dorothy. (1988.) "Sugar Taste Reception In Mammals." *Chemical Senses* 13(1):13-31.

Karp, H. (2001.) "The 'fourth trimester': A framework and strategy for understanding and resolving colic." *Contemporary Peds.* 21:92-114.

Landi, Val. (ed.) (2011.) "Stephen Hawking on non-carbon-based alien life." *The Daily Galaxy – Great Discoveries Channel.* https://dailygalaxy.com/2011/05/stephen-hawking-on-non-carbon-based-alien-life/

Lipman, E.A. and Grassi, J. R. (1942.) "Comparative auditory sensitivity of man and dog." *American Journal of Psychology* 55:84-89.

Marhold, S., Wiltschko, W. and Burda, H. (1997.) "A magnetic polarity compass for direction finding in a subterranean mammal." *Naturwissenschaften* 84(9):421–423. doi:10.1007/s001140050422

Mathger, L.M., Shashar, N. and Hanlon, R.T. (2009.) "Do cephalopods communicate using polarized light reflections from their skin?" *Journal of Experimental Biology* 212 (14): 2133–2140. doi:10.1242/jeb.020800

Meyers, Noel, Campbell, Neil A. and Reece, Jane B. (2005.) *Biology 7th Edition: Australian Version.* Pearson Education, Australia.

Meyers, Paul Z. (2014.) "Why do cavefish lose their eyes?" *ScienceBlogs.* https://scienceblogs.com/

pharyngula/2014/08/18/why-do-cavefish-lose-their-eyes

Moss, Laura. (2014.) "Do Foods Taste the Same to Animals As They Do To Us?" *Mother Nature Network.* http://www.mnn.com/earth-matters/animals/stories/do-foods-taste-the-same-to-animals-as-they-do-to-us

Nave, R. (2016.) "Transparency of water in the visible range." *HyperPhysics.* Department of Physics and Astronomy, Georgia State University. http://hyperphysics.phy-astr.gsu.edu/hbase/Chemical/watabs.html

Northeast Fisheries Science Center. (2011.) "NEFSC Fish FAQ." http://www.nefsc.noaa.gov/faq/fishfaq1b.html.

Pratchett, Terry. (1983 - 2015.) *Discworld.* Transworld Publishers, UK.

Reardon, Sara. (2014.) "Gut-brain link grabs neuroscientists." *Nature.* 515:175-7 doi:10.1038/515175a

Ritchison, Gary. (n.d.) "Comparative Vertebrate Anatomy - Skeletal Systems." *Department Of Biological Sciences, Eastern Kentucky University.* http://people.eku.edu/ritchisong/342notes2.htm.

Rowling, J. K. (2000). *Harry Potter and the Chamber of Secrets.* Scholastic, Inc., New York.

Sirucek, Stefan. (2013.) "Blue Blood Helps Octopus Survive Brutally Cold Temperatures."

National Geographic. http://newswatch.nationalgeographic.com/2013/07/10/blue-blood-helps-octopus-survive-brutally-cold-temperatures/

Speaks, Serpent. (2012.) "Blue Whales Bigger Than Dinosaurs?" *SerpentSpeaks.* http://serpentspeaks.wordpress.com/2012/09/30/blue-whales-bigger-than-dinosaurs/

The Wachowskis (dir.) (1999.) *The Matrix.* Warner Bros., USA.

Tolkien, J.R.R. (2001.) *The Return of The King: Being The Third Part of The Lord of The Rings.* Quality Paperback Book Club, New York.

Viegas, Jennifer. (2014.) "10 Best Sniffers in the Animal Kingdom." *Discovery News.* http://news.discovery.com/animals/10-best-sniffers-in-the-animal-kingdom-140722.htm

Warfield, D. (1973.) "The study of hearing in animals." In: Gay, W. (ed.), *Methods of Animal Experimentation, IV.* Academic Press, London, pp 43-143.

West, C.D. (1985.) "The relationship of the spiral turns of the cochela and the length of the basilar membrane to the range of audible frequencies in ground dwelling mammals". *Journal of the Acoustic Society of America* 77:1091-1101.

PART THREE: TINY LIFE

Doucleff, Michaeleen. (2018.) "Are There Zombie

Viruses In The Thawing Permafrost?" *MPRNews*. January 24.

Emmerich, Roland (dir.) (1996.) *Independence Day*. Centropolis Entertainment, USA.

New York State Government. (2018.) "Harmful Blue-green Algae: Frequently Asked Questions." *Department of Health.* https://www.health.ny.gov/environmental/water/drinking/bluegreenalgae/faq.htm

Meyers, Noel, Campbell, Neil A. and Reece, Jane B. (2005.) *Biology 7th Edition: Australian Version*. Pearson Education, Australia.

Milius, Susan. (2014.) "The Name Of The Fungus." *Science News*. 185(8). https://www.sciencenews.org/article/name-fungus.

Matt. (2018.) "Are Algae Plants?" In Defense of Plants. http://www.indefenseofplants.com/blog/2018/2/20/are-algae-plants

Peterson, Wolfgang (dir.) (1995.) *Outbreak*. Punch Productions, Inc, USA.

Wells, H.G. (1898.) *The War Of The Worlds*. William Heinemann, UK.

www.ingramcontent.com/pod-product-compliance
Lightning Source LLC
Chambersburg PA
CBHW071712020426
42333CB00017B/2240